Hertfordshire

COUNTRYSIDE BOOKS

NEWBURY, BERKSHIRE

Designed by Peter Davies, Nautilus Design
Produced through MRM Associates Ltd., Reading
Printed by Woolnough Bookbinding Ltd., Irthlingborough

CONTENTS

CONTENTS

Introduction

Writing this book has been rather like playing that game of choosing who, in history, you would like to invite for dinner. I think it would be a fascinating evening with these Hertfordshire heroes for company. Would William Leefe Robinson and Wulstan Tempest of the Royal Flying Corps discuss flying with Sir Geoffrey de Havilland, or would Robert Cecil, first Earl of Salisbury, catch up on royal affairs with Queen Elizabeth The Queen Mother? I'd like to talk to Lady Constance Lytton about her days with the suffragettes, thank Eric Morecambe for making me laugh, hear about the early days of silent films from John M. East, and share a glass or two with the indomitable Lady Elizabeth Cathcart. What a treat it would be.

All of the people in this book have excelled at what they did or have simply been larger than life – and sometimes both. They were not all born in Hertfordshire, or were lifelong inhabitants, but they all have a strong connection with us – we can surely claim, for instance, the two young pilots who shot Zeppelins down over Hertfordshire, while Earl Alexander of Tunis lived his life on the world stage but we can be honoured that he chose to be buried in the country churchyard at Ridge, near his family home.

Deciding who to include in a limited number of heroes is not as easy as it seems and I can only say, if I have left out someone you feel deserves to be here, that I chose those people whose stories particularly appealed to me. I hope they appeal to you too, and that you enjoy meeting some of the heroes of Hertfordshire.

Margaret Ward

Acknowledgements

With my thanks for the help and advice given by the following: Hertfordshire Archives & Local Studies; St Albans Library; Central Resources Library, Barnfield; the *Herts Advertiser*; *Hertfordshire Countryside*; David Cliff at Verulam Golf Club; Terry Pankhurst; Ian Simpson; Ralph Steiner at the de Havilland Aircraft Heritage Centre; the Henry Moore Foundation at Perry Green; and all those I have talked to about this book. More information about the people whose lives are described in *Hertfordshire Heroes* can be found in a wide variety of sources, including contemporary newspaper and magazine articles, biographical and autobiographical accounts, and websites.

1

Samuel Ryder (1858–1936)

The man behind the Ryder Cup

On 15th September 1985, over 20,000 spectators and millions of television viewers held their collective breath as Sam Torrance steadied himself for one of the most important putts of his golfing career. On the 17th green at The Belfry, Sutton Coldfield, he knew that holing the putt would square his match with American Andy North and give the European team victory in the Ryder Cup. When the ball rolled into the hole, the tears began to roll down Torrance's cheeks and he played, and won, the 18th in emotional turmoil. 'I've never known such a feeling,' he said afterwards. 'Everywhere I go, I'm the man who won the Ryder Cup. People stop me in the streets, call to me from cars. I've never known anything like it. Was the entire nation watching that putt?'

Perhaps not the entire nation, but certainly the Ryder Cup has achieved the status of a sporting event that enthralls even those who have no real interest in golf. It wasn't always so – the Cup has been played for by teams from Great Britain (Europe since 1979) and the United States every two years since 1927, but for many of those years the US was so dominant that only the keenest golfers could find it interesting as a competition. The 1985 win was the first time the US had been defeated in 28 years. Now, the game was on and Europe would never again be the under-dogs. With men like Severiano Ballasteros, Nick Faldo, Tony Jacklin, Bernhard Langer, Sandy Lyle, Ian Woosnam, Jose Maria Olazabal and many more, on our side, how could we lose?

The Ryder Cup itself is solid gold, with the figure of a golfer poised on the top. The model for the little figure was Abe Mitchell, said to be the greatest golfer never to win the Open and a close friend of the donor of the trophy – Samuel Ryder of St Albans. Sam's involvement with professional golf is extraordinary enough and well able to earn him the status of a hero of sport, but his story also reveals another claim to fame, for he was a champion of impoverished gardeners as well!

Samuel Ryder came to St Albans in 1895, aged 37, with a young family and a simple yet brilliant idea for a new business. His father was a successful nurseryman in Manchester and Samuel had worked for him in the family business for several years before seeking fresh experience in other parts of the country. Gardening was then well on its way to becoming the passion of the working class as well as the more wealthy middle class. People living in even the smallest of town cottages could find the space for a few flowers, or line up pots on the kitchen windowsill, while the demand for allotments was booming and local gardening clubs and societies were encouraging and educating their members. Yet suppliers had been slow to tap into demand and it was expensive to buy plants or to obtain seeds in small quantities. Samuel had an idea of how to satisfy this huge new market made up of customers who had little ready money but could afford a few pennies to buy their dreams in a packet of seeds.

So he settled in Hertfordshire, in a thriving market town, which offered excellent rail links with the rest of the country and was close to the capital. He spent time in St Albans' library going through trade directories and noting down names and addresses of individuals from the poorer parts of towns. He and his wife, Helen, then posted off a simple seed catalogue to each address, timing the posting so that it would arrive on a Saturday morning – hopefully the day when a working man would have a few hours

SAMUEL RYDER (1858–1936)

of leisure in which to peruse the catalogue and post back an order. Orders received by Samuel on Monday would be filled immediately and the customer would have his seeds in time to be out in the garden planting them on his next Saturday break.

Samuel called his new venture 'Ryder and Son', the name of his now-retired father's business, even though Samuel himself never had a son. His slogan from the beginning was: 'All seeds in penny packets from orchids to mustard and cress'. He aimed for a reliable, fast service and it was a success from the start. He sent out 250 catalogues on his first mailshot in 1895, working out of a room above a hatter's shop in High Street, St Albans, with the aid of one boy. Moving to successively larger premises over the next few years, by 1903 he was able to buy 27 Holywell Hill, next to the famed White Hart inn, and to create the largest warehouse complex in St Albans at the rear of the building. In 1911 he demolished the medieval building at No 27 and built the imposing edifice that stands today, adding an exhibition hall next door 20 years later (today the Café Rouge). He also somehow found the time in the 1920s to help his brother James set up the firm of Heath and Heather in St Albans, breaking new ground in the supply of herbal commodities and remedies.

Within 20 years of starting his penny-packet business, Samuel could boast of over a million catalogues sent out worldwide every year, offering over 5,000 varieties of seeds, with a workforce of some 90 local women who, in season, would post over 2,000 orders every day. He had begun his business at an ideal time and his fast, reliable service offered excellent quality and huge variety. Samuel himself travelled the world to find new plants and quality suppliers – one of the new arrivals in the garden border which he introduced from South Africa was the Livingstone Daisy, *Mesembryanthemum crinoflorium*. After Samuel's death, the firm was sold to R & G Cuthbert, and eventually became part of Suttons Seeds.

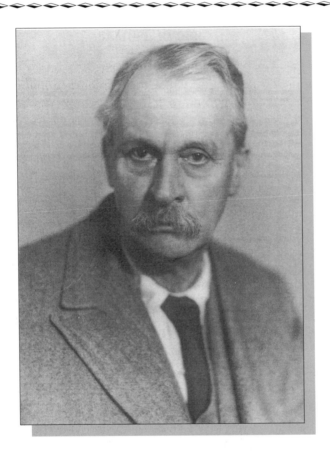

Sam Ryder.

Success brings money, but like many another successful businessman, Samuel did not always enjoy good health. A friend suggested he take up golf for fresh air and exercise. He became obsessed by the game. He laid out his own practice course in the paddock next to his home, Marlborough House, and in 1907 joined Verulam Golf Club, then only two years old. In 1911 he became Captain for the first time – he was Captain three times in all, and on the club committee for over 20 years. He also

SAMUEL RYDER (1858–1936)

employed the brilliant golfer Abe Mitchell as his private professional and this became a hugely successful partnership that would bring the Ryder Cup to the fore of the sporting world.

Samuel took a great interest in the game and frequently attended professional matches, getting to know the top golfers of the time such as the American champion, Walter Hagen. The more he talked to the professional golfers he met, the more he became concerned at the then lowly stature of the golfing professional. It seemed to him unfair that these dedicated and talented men should receive so little recognition, even having to take unpaid leave from their employing club if they wanted to play in competitions. The financial rewards were in any case small, even for those at the top. Samuel decided that what was needed was a competition of national interest, that would enhance their status in the eyes of both the public and their fellow golfers. He was no stranger to arranging international amateur matches at Verulam Golf Club.

The first, unofficial, match between Great Britain and the USA took place in June 1926 at Wentworth and aroused some interest in the national newspapers. The British team thrashed the Americans 13½ to 1½, and everyone enjoyed themselves hugely. In the club bar, almost immediately after the match, Samuel was involved in discussions as to whether this could be a regular fixture between the two countries. He had already offered to donate a gold cup to be played for, and so the Ryder Cup was born.

Samuel was delighted with the reaction to the competition, saying in 1931, 'I hope I have done several things in my life for the benefit of my fellow men but I am certain I have never done a happier thing than this.'

The first official Ryder Cup match therefore took place in America in 1927. The Americans won, and sadly that foretold the future course of events, America reaching such dominance that

HERTFORDSHIRE HEROES

Sam Ryder holding the Ryder Cup, with some of the members of the first British Ryder Cup team – left to right, F. Ray, C.A. Whitcombe, F. Robson, A.J. Havers, G. Gadd, A. Compston and G. Duncan.

the match eventually lost some of its interest to players and public alike. Then, in 1979, the Great Britain team became the European team and a new era was born. With it came increased money from sponsorship (though the players still receive no fee for competing), worldwide television coverage, intense rivalry, and sometimes a will to win that has spilled over into unsportsmanlike behaviour from spectators and players alike. It is a world away from the gentlemanly contest that Samuel Ryder created, and whether he would have totally approved has often been debated by journalists and players.

Golf and his seed business were only two facets of Samuel

SAMUEL RYDER (1858–1936)

Ryder's remarkable life. Somehow he also found the time to act as a Justice of the Peace, participate in religious activities, and take a full part in civic government, becoming a member of the Council in 1903 and elected Mayor of St Albans three times – you can still come across his name carved into the foundation stone of buildings in the city.

Sam Ryder died in a London hotel where he had spent Christmas with his family, on 2nd January 1936, and he is buried in St Albans cemetery, Fleetville. He was an uncommon man, who proved that success in business and sport could coincide with the notions of honesty and fair play. Deeply religious and solidly 'chapel', he still enjoyed a hot whisky toddy before bed and a glass of wine with dinner, and made an affable companion. Time and again in his life he proved that treating people well and honestly would pay off in the end, and as his daughter recalled, 'he had an enormous sense of pity and sympathy for the other chap'. With his bushy moustache and somewhat lugubrious appearance in photographs, he seems an unlikely hero, but his achievements were summed up at his funeral: 'He had the creative imagination and the spark of genius to build up his business, to win fame in the world of sport, to make great contributions to the life of St Albans, and to be prominent in so many forms of social service; but his real greatness lay in the fact that he extended that creative power to everything and to every person whom he met'.

2

Sir Harold Alexander (1891–1969)

A soldier to rank with the Duke of Wellington

In the tiny churchyard at Ridge, a small Hertfordshire village with sweeping views down across the Middlesex border towards London, lies one of the greatest soldiers of the 20th century, Field Marshal Earl Alexander of Tunis. That he should be buried here often comes as a surprise to people who may have come by accident across the plain and unassuming white stone slab that marks his grave, but the Hertfordshire connection with Alexander's family goes back over a century and a half.

Within the parish of Ridge, close to London Colney, is the manor of Tyttenhanger, which in the mid 19th century came into the possession of the Irish aristocratic family of the Earls of Caledon. Harold Rupert Leofric George Alexander was born in Ireland on 10th December 1891, third son of the 4th Earl of Caledon. His life was to be lived on a world stage but Tyttenhanger House, so convenient for London and yet so pleasantly peaceful, proved to be a special place for him and his family. The house that Alexander knew was built in the 17th century but those same advantages had once made Tyttenhanger a prized possession of the abbots of St Albans Abbey who built an earlier mansion here and laid out a deer park, as well as a place of refuge in times of trouble, notably for Henry VIII when plague forced him to flee London.

Alexander was destined, however, to make his career in the army, entering the Irish Guards in 1911. During the First World War he was wounded three times and awarded the Military Cross, the Distinguished Service Order, the French Legion of

SIR HAROLD ALEXANDER (1891–1969)

Honour and the Russian Order of St Anne. By 1917 he was acting lieutenant colonel commanding his battalion and he would later become one of the youngest major generals in the British Army. Between the wars he served in Ireland and India – he also married, to Lady Margaret Diana Bingham, daughter of the 5th Earl of Lucan. But it was the Second World War which was to bring the greatest challenges of his life, and to sweep him into the history books.

By 1942 the course of the Second World War was running anything but smoothly for the Allies. Their forces had enjoyed no major victories in battle against the German-Italian Axis armies in the three years since war was declared in September 1939. The whole of Europe was either allied to Hitler's Germany or occupied by his forces. In Russia the German army had advanced as far as Stalingrad. In the far east the Japanese had overrun the South Pacific, Hong Kong, Malaya and Burma. Britain itself had suffered the military and emotional turmoil of Dunkirk and the Battle of Britain, and was into its third grim year of aerial bombardment, U-boat blockade and rationing.

In North Africa the Allies' aim was always directed towards preventing the Axis forces taking control of the Suez Canal, the only sea route open into the Mediterranean. Since June 1940 the Western Desert Force (known as the Eighth Army from September 1941) had been tussling with Italian and German forces back and forth along the Mediterranean coastline of Egypt, Libya and Tunisia, but by August 1942 the tough Afrika Korps was winning the struggle under the leadership of the legendary General Edwin Rommel, forcing the Eighth Army hundreds of miles back deep into Egypt. The fall of Tobruk, a port on the Libyan coast, to Rommel in June that year had been a nasty psychological blow and now he was poised to push right through Allied lines to take Alexandria, Cairo and the Suez Canal.

Winston Churchill, Britain's Prime Minister and wartime leader,

Sir Harold Alexander in North Africa.

had no doubts about what must be done – the Eighth Army must strike back and destroy Rommel's army – but he had grown impatient with the lack of confidence shown by the commanders in Egypt and decided in a change in personnel at the very top. In came Lieutenant General Bernard Montgomery, 'Monty', as commander-in-chief of the Eighth Army. And in came General Sir Harold Alexander as overall Commander-in-Chief. Churchill made a special visit to Cairo in August 1942, to deliver a message to the new Commander-in-Chief of his army in the Middle East. 'Your prime and main duty,' he insisted, 'will be to take on and destroy at the earliest opportunity the German-Italian army commanded by Field Marshal Rommel together with all its supplies and establishments in Egypt and Libya.' He reckoned that he had found the men who could do it.

Now 51 years old, Alexander was an experienced soldier who

also possessed the personal qualities that brought him respect and loyalty from fellow officers and made him an ideal pairing with Monty, who was a down-to-earth character who excelled at leading from the front and inspiring his troops in a cause he made sure they understood. Alexander was confident, charming, sophisticated and tactful, with the ability to smooth out troubles and find a way through – his slogan 'Attack, attack, attack, even if you are on the defensive', must have warmed Churchill's heart. In 1939, commanding the 1st Division of the British Army, Alexander had fought the rearguard action at Dunkirk that brought enough time for thousands of men to be taken off the beaches and across the Channel back to England, living to fight another day. After that he had been in Burma, as Commander-in-Chief Southern Command, when once again he had had to get his men out and away in a difficult situation, this time faced by the Japanese invasion. Now, there would be no more retreating.

His task in Egypt in 1942 was to direct the coming battle behind the scenes and give all the support he could to the front line troops, while Monty led his men forward. On 19th August he gave instructions to Monty and the Eighth Army: 'prepare to attack the Axis forces with a view to destroying them at the earliest possible moment.'

Three months later – months of training and re-equipping, of renewing the morale of an army that had already been fighting for long months and had faced defeat – and finally after twelve days of hard and bitter fighting against an experienced and resourceful enemy, Monty and the Eighth Army defeated Rommel at El Alamein. It was a turning point in North Africa and also in the course of the whole war. At last we had a major victory and in England the church bells were rung in celebration, the first time they had sounded since Dunkirk. As Churchill summed it up: 'Before Alamein we never had a victory. After Alamein we never had a defeat.'

The impetus of war now lay in Alexander's hands as Monty's

men pushed on along the coast. Meanwhile, at the other end of the African coastline, in French Morocco and Algeria, Operation Torch got under way with an invasion by Allied and US forces fighting together under General Dwight D. Eisenhower. In January 1943 Alexander was made deputy to Eisenhower, now Supreme Commander of Allied forces in North Africa. Their next objective was Tunis, and Alexander was given command of the Eighth Army and all the land forces in Tunisia.

Monty and the Eighth Army fought their way along the coastal plain, mile by mile, through the heat of the day, the cold nights, the endless sands that turned into a quagmire when it rained, and attacks by a courageous enemy with the continual worry of maintaining a supply line across inhospitable country. At the same time, the British First Army, American II Corps and Free French forces were approaching from the east, tightening the noose that lay around Tunis. On 12th May 1943, the enemy surrendered and the war in North Africa was over. Alexander sent a message to Churchill: 'Sir, it is my duty to report that the Tunisian campaign is over. All enemy resistance has ceased. We are masters of the North African shores.'

Not that his war was over yet, by a long way. From North Africa into Sicily and on to the Italian mainland, destination Rome, Alexander oversaw some of the most ferocious fighting of the war, including the storming of Monte Cassino in May 1944 when he was C.-in-C. Allied Armies in Italy. A few months later he was appointed Supreme Allied Commander Mediterranean, and had been made a Field Marshal. His persistence in pursuing the enemy northwards through Italy paid off at last, when in May 1945 he became the first Allied commander to take the large-scale surrender of enemy troops in Europe.

It had taken two years and eight months of some of the hardest fighting our armies had encountered, and cost the lives of some 200,000 British soldiers. When Alexander was elevated in the

SIR HAROLD ALEXANDER (1891–1969)

peerage on 1st March 1946, it was as Viscount Alexander of Tunis, in honour of the men who had fought his greatest campaign. 'Always at the back of my mind when I make plans is the thought that I am playing with human lives,' he told war correspondents. 'Good chaps get killed or wounded and it is a terrible thing. The proudest thing I can say is that I am a front-line soldier. I fought with my battalion of Guards and was wounded three times, so I know what it means and I do not throw away lives unless it is absolutely necessary.'

After the war he was also honoured by the United States, the USSR, Greece and Poland. He might have gone on to become chief of the Imperial General Staff, but Churchill had a more important job for him to do and for the next five years he was the King's representative as Governor General of Canada. He had, after all, proved his qualifications for diplomacy as he tried to keep the peace between Allied and American officers as they fought together from Africa to Rome!

Life in Canada was busy, but he could take the opportunity to wind down a little and indulge in his own interests – painting, for instance, which was a passion with him, and playing sports. He even, apparently, personally supervised the tapping of the maple trees at Rideau Hall, the Governor General's residence, for maple syrup. The Canadians loved their new Governor General, a charismatic war hero who had the gift of being able to communicate with people, and he is still remembered as one of the most popular figures of post-war Canada.

In 1952 he took the path of many an ex-soldier and became a politician. Churchill wanted him back in London as Minister of Defence, but he was not happy in the post. His tendency to speak off the cuff was loved by the Canadians, but was not so popular in Whitehall and, as The Times noted: 'It is fair to say that he never fathomed the natures or motives of politicians.' In 1954 he handed the post over to Harold Macmillan and retired from political life.

Over the next few years he was kept busy with a variety of official appointments, from Constable of the Tower of London to President of the MCC. Typically, he made an enthusiastic president of the Anglo-German Association from 1958, and after his death his 'chivalrous and Christian attitude' was praised by the men who had once been his enemies.

Field Marshal, Earl Alexander of Tunis, KG, PC, GCB, OM, GCMG, CSI, DSO, MC, died on 16th June 1969, aged 77. His funeral took place at St George's Chapel, Windsor – 'a funeral service of military perfection, splendid in colour and ceremony' attended by dignitaries from all over the world. Yet it was in the small, peaceful country churchyard of St Margaret's at Ridge that Alexander chose to be buried. He was laid there on 25th June 1969, attended only by his family. Often Remembrance Day poppies mark the spot, placed there by old soldiers who have good cause to remember a man once compared to another great commander, the Duke of Wellington.

Alexander's grave in Ridge churchyard.

3

Florence Barclay (1862–1921)

Author who sold a million books

In 1909 a romantic novel called *The Rosary* became an instant bestseller in Britain and the USA. By the time its author died in 1921 well over a million copies had been sold worldwide, translated into eight languages. It was written by a 48-year-old vicar's wife from Hertford Heath – Florence Louisa Barclay. When her ship steamed into New York Harbour in 1910, she was mobbed by fans, reporters and photographers, and the American customs officers waved her through – 'the luggage of the author of *The Rosary* need not be examined'! To say that Florence's life had taken an unexpected turn would be an understatement.

When Florence had settled into the vicarage in Hertford Heath in 1881 as the wife of the new vicar, she was only eighteen years old. A clergyman's daughter, brought up in vicarages in Limpsfield, Surrey and Limehouse in the East End of London, she had married her father's curate, the Reverend Charles Barclay, a few months before. She was a beautiful young woman, energetic, kind, practical, and a great organiser. A Victorian vicar's wife could be as important to the parish as the vicar himself and Florence found plenty of scope in their new home for her own considerable abilities.

Simply running her home life at the vicarage might have seemed enough work for one woman. Not only did she have one of those vast Victorian vicarages to keep, admittedly with the aid of servants, but by the time she was 23, in 1886, she had five small children, and another three completed her family of eight by 1900. She was so young that she could have been mistaken for her children's elder sister at times, particularly when she was playing in the garden in a simple white dress, 'her thick dark hair tied back in a coil on her shoulders'. Loved and secure, the children never had the sense that they were in any way neglected, despite their mother's extraordinarily busy life.

People who met Florence seemed to sense that she had a genuine passion for everything she undertook, underpinned by her deep Christian faith. Despite her youth she was soon organising the members of her husband's flock and one of the first things she undertook was a bible class for men on a Sunday afternoon, an informal little gathering with a hymn or two as well. It became enormously popular, so that soon she had over 100 men attending every Sunday and a number walked miles out from Hertford to be there. That class continued for the next 30 years.

The same men probably attended the 'entertainment' in the Mission Room on a Friday night. Hertford Heath wasn't the only place in Victorian Hertfordshire where there was concern over the ease with which a working man's weekly wage disappeared in an hour or two in the local inn, leaving little for his wife to spend on food at market the next day. Florence's solution was to offer an alternative to the pub – which was otherwise the only place men could meet socially – in a free evening of songs and humour. It was packed every Friday and ran a different programme each week, the villagers performing for each other; the blacksmith was a hit singing the popular song *The Village Blacksmith*, brandishing the hammer he used in the forge. Florence noticed that the words of songs had become garbled over the years: 'Sometimes the words, passed on by word of mouth, had lost all sense, but no one seemed to mind.' How else to explain the surreal ditty: 'And I took the morning train / Across the raging main . . .'?

The women of the parish found that Florence had just as much care for them. Almost all of them were members of her Mothers'

FLORENCE BARCLAY (1862-1921)

Meeting, for instance, which included a system of buying materials wholesale and retailing it to the women, who could pay by weekly instalments. She also formed a women's cricket club and played matches every week in season, and taught a regular women's physical training class long before it was thought good, or even proper, for women to take exercise. Florence had no doubt that women were able to do whatever they were called on to do, and later became the first President of the East Herts Women's Voters Association.

She spent a great deal of time in organising the music for the church. She had a beautiful contralto voice and as a girl had hoped to train as a singer. Now she could teach others to sing, and she formed a strong choir which eventually was successful enough to give concerts at county venues such as Hertford Corn Exchange, Ware Town Hall and Haileybury College. Every Sunday she played the organ for the church services.

And still, she had energy to spare. She loved to walk for miles, to play sports, or to bicycle. In fact, it was a bicycle ride that changed her life.

One day she cycled from Hertford Heath to Cromer, in Norfolk, and back, a distance of about 120 miles. That epic bike ride weakened her heart and laid her low for several months. During her early convalescence, forbidden to sit up or to undertake any activity, she spent hours creating a story in her mind and when at last she was allowed to be raised in bed a little, she couldn't wait to write it all down. She called the story *The Rosary*, after a once-popular song that her heroine, Jane, sings in the book.

Florence had enjoyed writing as a child but her only effort as an adult had been a short story written for her own amusement in 1905: *The Wheels of Time*. The personalities she created then so took over her mind that one night, travelling home in the train from London to Hertford, she had written a complete love scene between her two main characters, Jane and Garth. Her illness

Florence Barclay in 1912, at the height of her popularity.

gave her the leisure and time to do the rest. There it might have ended, as a purely private family amusement, had her sister in America not loved the stories and taken them to Putnam's publishing house. In 1909 *The Rosary* was published both here and in New York and the rest, as they say, is history.

Florence wrote another nine novels after the success of *The*

FLORENCE BARCLAY (1862–1921)

Rosary – The Mistress of Shenstone (1910), *The Following of the Star* (1911), *Through the Postern Gate* (1912), *The Upas Tree* (1912), *The Broken Heart* (1913), *The Wall of Partition* (1914), *My Heart's Right There* (1914), *In Hoc Vince* (1915) and *The White Ladies of Worcester* (1917). Each one enhanced her reputation as a popular writer and she became nationally famous and recognised wherever she went. The books were cleverly marketed with purple covers, easily picked out in a bookshop window, and her fans readily associated that colour with their favourite author – on that New York harbourside in 1910, a large purple banner with gold lettering fluttered to greet her arrival in America. Two of the books were adapted as silent films: *The Mistress of Shenstone* and *The Rosary*.

Florence continued to suffer bouts of ill health. One curious incident could almost have come from one of her books. In 1912 she was injured in a car accident, a blow to the head causing a cerebral haemorrhage and giving her such great pain that for a time her family and doctors feared she would never recover her mental capacity. Then, when out in a boat at Keswick with friends, she was accidentally hit on the head again with an oar – and in the best traditions of romantic fiction, she made a complete recovery and was once more her old self.

Throughout the years of her fame, both here in England and over in America, she travelled on speaking tours, gave interviews, wrote articles, answered every letter from her fans, and visited bookshops to personally thank booksellers for their support – all this in addition to continuing to support her husband at home in Hertford Heath. After the war, however, illness forced her to retreat from public life. In 1921 her husband resigned his living at Hertford Heath and, after nearly 40 years, they left Hertfordshire to return to Surrey and her childhood surroundings. She may have suspected that it would not be for long – in March that year she prepared herself for an operation, but died under the anaesthetic at the age of 59. She was buried at Limpsfield, where she had grown up.

The Barclays were long remembered with great affection in Hertford Heath; 'a very handsome pair', recalled one elderly parishioner. Florence's last gift to the village was the war memorial cross. All through the war she and her husband had held a short service each day in the church which had given great comfort to villagers worried about their sons, brothers or fathers at the front in France, and Florence's war work had been personal and quietly done, visiting the bereaved and the wounded in hospital. She wanted the village's war dead to have a greater memorial than the simple plaque in the church which was all that could be afforded by the parishioners themselves, and the unveiling of the cross at the entrance to the village was her last public appearance before her death.

Tastes in fiction change and it's doubtful whether Florence's books would find much of an audience today, but in her own time she wrote stories that enthralled her readers. One critic, J.C. Squire, said that 'she knows how to serve out the glamour and the pathos with a ladle . . . Though on all sides the blood rains down in torrents, love's interests still are in safe hands with Florence.' She would have liked that. Her Christian faith, and the belief that love and right would triumph, was always the bedrock of her writing and her stories had a moral, but it was one which encouraged people to be better than they were, to strive harder to find the right way to live, and to live with courage and optimism. Much of the money she earned, she quietly gave away. When she gave a talk, she spoke about faith, God and the Bible rather than herself and her books. She never became 'literary', that was not her style. She simply touched the hearts of people all over the world, and perhaps that is the epitaph she would have chosen for herself.

4

Lady Elizabeth Bowes-Lyon (1900–2002)

Queen Elizabeth The Queen Mother

Elizabeth Bowes-Lyon neither expected, nor wanted, to become Queen. Only the abdication of a King, something which had not happened for over 600 years, propelled her and her shy, stammering Bertie to the throne of Great Britain. But in her amazing life that spanned a century she met her destiny with all the charm, warmth, and steel resolve of which she was capable. Needless to say, she was a Hertfordshire girl.

On 4 August 1900 the Honourable Elizabeth Angela Marguerite Bowes-Lyon was born. She was the youngest daughter of Lord and Lady Glamis, ninth of ten children, and her birth certificate plainly states that she was born at St Paul's Walden Bury in Hertfordshire. There has been some dispute about the accuracy of this information over the years, and Palace publicity merely says that she 'spent her early childhood' in the county, but local people will have no truck with the idea that she might have actually been born in London. There is a plaque on the wall of the church at St Paul's Walden that records her birth and baptism there, erected in the 1920s, and that is good enough for us.

There is a great deal of misty nostalgia over that long Edwardian summer before the outbreak of the First World War, but this little girl had an almost idyllic childhood. The family (her father had inherited the title of 14th Earl of Strathmore and Kinghorne in 1904) moved, as aristocratic families did then and had done for centuries, between their properties throughout the year, so that summers would be spent in Scotland at Glamis Castle, the 'season' in London, and Christmas and springtime at St Paul's

Walden Bury. She was a beautiful little girl, adored by her family and those who worked for them, kind-hearted and fun-loving. She had pets galore to play with, a pony to ride, and a younger brother, David, to boss around. Sadly, that world ended forever on her fourteenth birthday, when war was declared between England and Germany. A year later came the news that her elder brother, Fergus, had been killed on the Western Front.

When the war ended, Lady Elizabeth was eighteen years old. Now a beautiful young woman who loved to dance, she and her friends welcomed the start of the jazz age, when some of the darkness of five years of devastating war could be danced away. She moved in the kind of circles that interacted with the Royal Family of King George V and Queen Mary, and was a bridesmaid at the wedding of Princess Mary. She was in demand and popular, and settling down in marriage was probably the last thing on her mind.

So when the quiet, shy Duke of York, second son of the King and Queen, asked her to marry him, she refused. He asked again, and again, and at last she accepted, while walking with him in the gardens at St Paul's Walden Bury. Her family were pleased, his family were delighted, and HRH Prince Albert Frederick Arthur George, known to his friends as 'Bertie', knew he had gained a pearl above price. The love affair, when made public, lifted hearts everywhere. 'The Royal Love Romance. Woodland Wooing in Hertfordshire', announced the *Hertfordshire Mercury* that January in 1923. 'The engagement,' they reported the Earl as saying, 'did not take us altogether by surprise.'

Elizabeth's hesitation was natural. She was no stranger to the lives of the Royal Family and understood that she would have to endure a goldfish-bowl public life with them – nothing, of course, compared to today's media coverage, but intrusive enough even then to be sometimes disturbing. She also realised that marriage to Bertie would mean providing the support he needed to cope

LADY ELIZABETH BOWES-LYON (1900–2002)

with life out of the Services as second in line to the throne. For he suffered from a quite severe speech impediment that made talking in public an agony – radio recordings during his reign confirm that his stammer was at times quite intense, a terrible burden for anyone forced to make speeches. She could never have dreamed, however, that in just a few years he was going to need all the help and support she could muster.

Elizabeth and Albert were married on 26th April 1923 at Westminster Abbey, and Elizabeth made her first public appearance as Duchess of York a couple of months later at the RAF Pageant at Hendon. The newspapers welcomed this new face and dubbed her 'the smiling Duchess'. After the stiff formality of the King and Queen she was a ray of warm sunshine in a grey and hard world of economic depression, unemployment and poverty. She gave herself wholeheartedly to whatever she was called on to do, and charmed people with her enthusiasm and knack of making every individual feel special. Amongst the public appearances and overseas tours of those inter-war years, she also made the first of many visits back to Hertfordshire, both personal and official – opening the new cottage hospital at Welwyn in 1934 was just one event, amongst the other opening ceremonies, the presentation of medals and awards, and the laying of foundation stones and planting of trees.

She and Bertie enjoyed a happy, comfortable family life. Their first daughter, Elizabeth, was born on 21st April 1926, and Margaret on 21st August 1930. When they all stayed at the Bury with her brother, they were able to pop into Hitchin to shop, just as she had as a child. Her children enjoyed life at the Bury as much as she had always done and the familiar places and people had a special place in her heart.

When George V died in 1936, Bertie's older brother succeeded to the throne as King Edward VIII. Edward was as unlike his brother as it was possible to be – he loved the glamour of being king, mixing with the rich and famous and notorious and living the 'fast life' as hard as he could. But he had a weakness about him too, which meant that when he fell in love with an American divorcee called Mrs Wallis Simpson, he could not contemplate life without her, and failed to understand why the Establishment and government did not see things in the same way. It was unthinkable then for the King of England to marry a divorced woman, and the fact that she was also American did not endear her to the general public. Months of secret talks went on between the King, the Prime Minister, Stanley Baldwin, the other members of the Royal Family and government ministers, but the King refused to bend – he would have Wallis or they could not have him as their King, that was his final word. Finally, the decision was made, and in a famous radio broadcast Edward gave up his throne for the woman he loved.

Edward abdicated on 11th December 1936, and Bertie – taking his fourth given name – was proclaimed King George VI. At the Coronation on 12th May 1937, he looked solemn, almost sad at times, and weighed down by the Crown placed upon his head. Elizabeth's life had changed irrevocably, and so had that of her children – her ten year old daughter was now first in line to the throne. It was enough to shake anyone. Throughout it all, the new Queen Consort maintained silence and a serene smile, but she never forgave the woman who, she felt, had created the whole sorry situation – Wallis Simpson, now married to her ex-king and styled Duchess of Windsor. Even when they were both old ladies, Elizabeth could not forget that her dear Bertie had been pushed into a situation for which he had no taste and no inclination, and which she felt had shortened his life.

Not for the first time, or the last, the Royal Family had to collectively pull up its socks and recreate public support and respect after a somewhat tawdry episode. George and Elizabeth would succeed in doing so through hard work and a commitment

LADY ELIZABETH BOWES-LYON (1900–2002)

to 'duty' that impressed their subjects. When George was proclaimed King, he pledged to 'work above else for the welfare of the British Commonwealth of Nations'. That pledge came from the heart, and has been kept by his daughter, Queen Elizabeth II.

It was the family's actions during the Second World War that really embedded Elizabeth in British hearts. When the Blitz on London and other major cities began in 1940, the Royal Family stayed put. A suggestion that the two girls should be sent to Canada out of harm's way met with short shrift: 'The children won't go without me. I won't leave the King. And the King will never leave.'

All through that terrible time, and those to come, Elizabeth was at George's side as he toured the country, clambering over the rubble of bombed-out houses, stopping to talk to firemen, policemen, air raid wardens, ambulance men and women, the neighbours and the bereaved. Their visits to Hertfordshire were typical, visiting wounded servicemen at the military hospitals set up at the Bury and at Hatfield House, and stopping off at Letchworth to meet factory workers. Above all, they were seen to be *there* – a huge morale booster that is still recalled by the now older generation who lived through those years. And when Buckingham Palace was bombed, while the family were in residence, she greeted it with a kind of relief. At last, she said, she could look the East End in the face. Now they really were all in it together.

In 1948, on their silver wedding anniversary, King George paid public tribute to the strength and inspiration that Elizabeth had brought to their marriage. Four years later, she was a widow. After months of illness, and the removal of a lung, George died at Sandringham on 6th February 1952, and was buried in St George's Chapel, Windsor. He was only 56.

Elizabeth moved out of Buckingham Palace and into Clarence House, where she would live for the next 50 years. Her daughter,

Elizabeth, was now Queen, and she took the title of Queen Elizabeth The Queen Mother. 'My only wish', she had said after her husband's death, 'is to continue the work we sought to do together.' And so she did.

During the next half century, Elizabeth became the 'Queen Mum' to millions all over the world – an instantly recognisable figure, whose penchants for horse racing and the odd glass of gin were common knowledge and endearing. Her royal duties were never ending, even as she got older, and included over 40 official visits abroad, patronage or presidency of over 350 organisations, and myriad official functions. In Hertfordshire, to mention only a few, she opened Hitchin School for Girls in 1955, came to Hertford Grammar School's 350th anniversary celebrations, visited the very new Stevenage New Town in 1956, was made an Honorary Freeman of St Albans in 1961, opened the Queen Mother Theatre in Hitchin in 1983, went to pageants and school prizegivings, visited the Gardens of the Rose at Chiswell Green, and appeared at Welwyn Garden City's Golden Jubilee celebrations in 1970. She was also commander-in-chief to several regiments, including the old Hertfordshire Regiment (TA) and the Bedfordshire & Hertfordshire Regiment, later the Anglian Regiment when service cuts and mergers took place. The list goes on and on. Look through old copies of any local newspaper and there she is, always gracious, always with a gentle smile for the photographer and the people who have come to see her, never caught unawares with a bored or tired look on her face. In fact, the complete professional that she undoubtedly was.

There were efforts, particularly in later years, to tar her with the same brush that came into use when some sections of the media decided that the younger royals were not worth the money we spend on them. She would probably have agreed, at times – she often watched the activities of the new generation with some distress and anger that the old concepts of duty and responsibility

LADY ELIZABETH BOWES-LYON (1900–2002)

*Queen Elizabeth The Queen Mother at the opening of the de Havilland
Mosquito Aircraft Museum at Salisbury Hall in 1984.
(de Havilland Aircraft Heritage Centre)*

seemed no longer in vogue. She certainly seems to have had her problems with Princess Diana, who in so many ways went through the kind of transformation that she herself had done, but her love and support for her favourite grandson, Prince Charles, were constants in both their lives.

As time went on we celebrated her 80th, then her 90th, and then her 100th birthdays. There were a few health scares – a stuck fishbone, a hip replacement . . . but time and time again the press and television obituaries that had been in preparation for years were shelved once more. It began to seem almost as if she might go on forever. Then suddenly it was over, catching even television newsmen by surprise, after a dreadful few months in which she lost her younger daughter, Princess Margaret.

The decision was made for her coffin to lie in state at Westminster Hall from Friday, 5th April 2002 to the morning of Tuesday, 9th April, when it would be taken to Westminster Abbey for the funeral service. What a waste of time, said some, nobody will come, the days are over when people wanted to line past a royal coffin, the Royal Family aren't that popular anymore. But now Elizabeth surprised the chattering classes once again. Over 200,000 people, from small children to pensioners, queued to walk slowly past her coffin and pay their last respects. The hours the Hall were open had to be extended to 21 a day to cope with the numbers and at one time people were standing patiently in the queue outside for up to ten hours, the line stretching three miles back to the Millennium Bridge. The most poignant moment came when her four grandsons – the Prince of Wales, the Duke of York, the Earl of Wessex and Viscount Linley – took up their posts at each corner of her coffin, to keep the 'Princes' Vigil'.

It was an incredible life, which we can justly claim began in a Hertfordshire village and during which she retained a special affection for the surroundings of her childhood. Without her the Royal Family might have foundered after Edward VIII's abdication, but with her they gained a woman who was, in the words of her grandson, Prince Charles, 'one of the most remarkable and wonderful people in the world'.

5

Lady Elizabeth Cathcart (1691–1789)

A Gothic heroine

Sometimes the truth really is stranger than fiction. The life of Lady Cathcart of Tewin Water was so bizarre that you would be forgiven for thinking it was merely the plot for a Gothic novel – and in fact it was immortalised in part in a famous early 19th-century story, *Castle Rackrent*, by the Irish writer, Maria Edgeworth. Yet this gutsy woman survived all that life could throw at her and had the last laugh in the end.

She was born Elizabeth Malyn, the daughter of a London brewer with property in Southwark and Battersea, at the end of the 17th century – about 1691 or 1692, we aren't quite sure. Elizabeth married four times in her long and eventful life, three times acquiring wealth and property and the last time nearly losing all she had.

James Fleet Esq., her first husband, she may have married for love, or it may have been to please her parents, as she later said. He was a wealthy man, the son and heir of Sir John Fleet of the City of London who had been Lord Mayor in 1693. As well as property in London, he owned the manor of Tewin in Hertfordshire and during their marriage he and Elizabeth spent time and money rebuilding and 'beautifying' Tewin Water House, which was set in its own parkland. When he died in 1733, aged 47, he left the house to his widow.

Elizabeth very rapidly married again, in 1734. This time, she said, it was for money. Her second husband was a Hertfordshire neighbour Captain William Sabine, the younger brother of General the Hon. Joseph Sabine of nearby Tewin House (though

Tewin Water, where Lady Cathcart lived and
where she returned in triumph from her ordeal.
(Hertfordshire Archives & Local Studies)

some accounts have Queenhoo Hall as the Sabine home). That marriage was brief – William died four years later, and presumably left Elizabeth a little wealthier than she had been before.

The third marriage was for a title, and the lucky man in 1739 was the Rt. Hon. Charles, eighth Lord Cathcart, a Scotsman and a distinguished soldier who in 1740 was made Commander-in-Chief of the British forces in the West Indies, where we were fighting the Spanish. On the voyage out to join his troops, he died suddenly. Lady Cathcart donned widow's weeds again.

This unlucky marital record might have been enough for some women. Elizabeth, now in her late forties, had property, money and a title, and no man to tell her what to do. She divided her time between Hertfordshire and Lord Cathcart's town house in

Westminster and prepared to enjoy herself. Later she would say that her fourth marriage came about because 'the devil owed her a grudge and would punish her for her sins'. Handsome Hugh Maguire was certainly sent by the devil.

At some time in the years following Lord Cathcart's death, Elizabeth met this charming Irish adventurer, perhaps when she was taking the waters at fashionable Bath. Maguire was a few years her junior, a younger son of a landed family in Ireland who had spent time on the Continent in the Austrian army. Elizabeth was taken by him and set him up as a lieutenant colonel in the British army, this being a time when a commission could be easily bought if you had the money and influence. She married him on 18th May 1745, and brought him home to Hertfordshire.

When did she realise that it was a case of the biter bit, that Maguire wanted only her money and could well do without her? Back in the 18th century, the moment a woman married all that she possessed became her husband's and Elizabeth must have been suspicious even before they wed because she took the trouble to have a marriage settlement drawn up which protected her wealth, she thought, from her lover.

For a year the couple lived at Tewin Water. Elizabeth must now have had serious doubts about her husband's intentions because she decided that he was not going to get his hands on her jewellery, at least. She had some of her jewels plaited into her hair (probably her wig hair, as it was the fashion of the time to wear an elaborate wig over one's own hair) and others sewn into her quilted petticoats. To do so, she must have had to trust at least one servant not to give her secret away and the household seems to have been split between 'her' staff and Maguire's.

One day in September 1746 Maguire took Elizabeth out in the coach for 'an airing'. Before they set off Elizabeth ordered two geese to be prepared for dinner. That was the last her servants would see of her for the next twenty years.

Elizabeth became alarmed when the coachman drove on far beyond a distance when they would be able to return to Tewin Water by dinnertime. Maguire would only say that they were on their way to Chester, 'and to Chester they should go', but she must have suspected that Ireland was their destination and that Maguire had shown his true colours at last.

When no one appeared for dinner, the servants back at Tewin Water sat down and ate the geese themselves. A few hours later, two of Maguire's men arrived and proceeded to strip the house of its silver and china, the best furniture, even the horses in the stables. They told the household staff that the Maguires had been unexpectedly called to Oxford, where the master's mother was dying, and that Elizabeth wanted her possessions with her as she might be some time away – nobody believed a word of it.

Once the news got out, Elizabeth's friends and relatives sent an attorney riding after the couple on the Chester road with a writ of *habeus corpus*. He caught up with them at an inn at Chester, but Maguire had a cool head and may have foreseen that this would happen. The attorney did not actually know Elizabeth by sight, and had no cause to doubt that the woman he was introduced to was indeed Maguire's wife. It seems likely it was one of his mistresses instead, who coolly told the attorney that she was travelling with her husband of her own free will. What could the attorney do but bow, apologise and depart? And just in case he became a little suspicious as he rode home and decided to come back again, Maguire sent a band of roughs after him to rob him and take his papers which they brought back to the inn.

So Elizabeth was spirited away to Ireland. Once in Dublin, Maguire forced her to sign a deed that turned the control of her property over to him. Then he took her to his own house, Tempo Manor in County Fermanagh, and settled down to live as he pleased. He rapidly became known locally as 'the wicked colonel', and his drunken, bawdy behaviour was notorious.

Elizabeth was kept locked in a room, incredibly, for the next twenty years; it is apparently still to be seen at Tempo Manor estate. No one came to her aid and no one was about to risk the wrath of Maguire, a noted shot and always ready to call a man out for a duel. He kept her hungry and cold. When the deep-drinking, neighbouring gentry came to dinner, he would mock her by sending a servant out to her with his compliments, saying that they would drink her Ladyship's health and asking if there was anything she would like to eat. 'Lady Cathcart's compliments, and she has everything she needs,' would come back the reply.

Her wits did not desert her. At some point she managed to smuggle out her jewels, thanks to an honest woman called Mrs Johnson, so that Maguire never got his hands on them.

The manner of Maguire's death is a mystery. Some say he died in a duel, which is what happened to his fictional counterpart in *Castle Rackrent*, but there is also a different and more satisfying tale. In that version, Maguire discovered that Elizabeth had secreted the deeds to her property behind the wooden wall panelling at Tewin Water. He went straight there, but was unable to open the hidden door because the lock had rusted over. When he tried to force the panel with a knife, it slipped and cut his hand. Lockjaw, or tetanus, killed him within a few weeks.

After twenty years of imprisonment, Elizabeth was released in about 1764, 'ragged, half-starved and almost deranged'. That she had survived at all was amazing, but she was a tough old bird, now in her sixties, and her wits were soon as sharp as ever. She returned to Tewin Water, to the delight of her servants and the neighbourhood, where she wasted no time in ejecting Maguire's tenant, Mr Joseph Steele. He tried to resist, but might as well have given in – she took him to court and appeared in person at the Hertfordshire assizes, winning her case and her property.

Before she married the wicked colonel, Elizabeth had had a ring engraved with the words: 'If I survive I will have five', which seems to suggest that she knew she was taking a dangerous decision when she wed Number Four. She never did make it five, but she had fun trying. She is said to have danced at Welwyn 'with the spirit of a young woman' when she was over 80 years old.

In 1783 some of her property, including the Tewin manor, was sold in chancery, suggesting that she had danced a fair proportion of her money away as well. A fortune must have been wasted by Maguire too, and the estate in Ireland was heavily in debt to her trustees after her death; in 1799 they forced the sale of the property away from the Maguire family.

Elizabeth died on 3rd August 1789, in her 98th year. She had wanted a quiet funeral but her story had become so well known by then that people flocked to be there. The *Gentleman's Magazine* describes the scene: 'Her body was dressed in linen, and laid in a leaden coffin; the outside coffin was covered with velvet, trimmed with gold, on which was a gold plate, whereon were engraven the names of her husbands, her age, etc. She was carried in a hearse and six, followed by two coaches and six, and a prodigious concourse of people, to the church of Tewin, where she was buried in a vault near her first husband. Hat-bands and gloves were given in general to all who chose to attend, and a sumptuous entertainment was provided for them.'

Apart from some legacies to poor people in the parish and to a few relations, what she had, she mainly left to her domestic staff – her 'cook-maid' was to get the contents of the scullery and kitchen, her dairymaid all the cattle and poultry, the gardener the garden tools and, with the footman, all the beer in the cellar, and so on. The labourers on the estate were to divide up the pigs and sheep between them, and she even left money to buy coal to heat the old village school, which is today a private house.

LADY ELIZABETH CATHCART (1691–1789)

Tewin Water House was extensively rebuilt in 1798 and in the 1950s became a school for deaf children. In Tewin church, however, you can still see Elizabeth's memorial, a plaque on the wall that records she was 'sometime the wife of James Fleet, esq., of Tewin Water, but afterwards the widow of the Right Hon. Lord Cathcart'. Of the wicked colonel there is no mention.

Lady Cathcart's memorial in Tewin church

6

Robert Cecil (1563–1612)

Counsellor to kings and builder of Hatfield House

'The name of my successor is like the tolling of my own death bell.' For years before her death in 1603 Elizabeth I refused to even consider the prospect that her life would one day end, while for her courtiers even to discuss the succession to the throne was an invitation to step over the line into treason. Yet one man with a deep family loyalty to his Queen worked secretly for years to make sure that after her death there would be no uncertainty, no threat of riot or chaos, no cause for armed factions to come to blows, and his achievement in bringing the country through those dangerous days was one of the greatest of his career. He was Robert Cecil, first of the Earls of Salisbury and builder of Hertfordshire's greatest treasure, Hatfield House.

Hatfield was a special place for the Cecils, and for the Tudor monarchs they served. The great Bishop's Palace, built during the 1490s, was a royal residence in the 16th century – here the Princesses Mary and Elizabeth lived while Anne Boleyn was Henry VIII's wife, and Elizabeth found refuge here while her brother Edward and sister Mary reigned in their turn. Elizabeth was at Hatfield on 17th November 1558 when the news was brought that Mary was dead and that she was now Queen. She held the first Privy Council meeting of her long reign here in Hertfordshire, in the familiar surroundings of the house where she had grown up. Yet despite this glittering royal history, it was to be Robert Cecil who would make Hatfield his own and whose influence can still be felt today.

ROBERT CECIL (1563-1612)

Robert Cecil, 1st Earl of Salisbury.

Cecil could be said to have been born into the Queen's service. He was the second son of William Cecil, Lord Burghley, who was known to many of his contemporaries as 'The Fox' and was Elizabeth's loyal and trusted advisor for 40 years. Burghley's eldest son, Thomas, showed no sign of following in his father's footsteps and all Burghley's hopes rested on Robert as his political heir. He gave him every opportunity to soak up both academic knowledge and the kind of political savvy that can only come from observing those in power at close quarters.

In an age of virile, glamorous adventurers, Robert Cecil stood out. He was small and slightly hunch-backed, and walked with a halting, splay-footed gait. By the side of courtiers like Sir Walter Raleigh or the Earl of Essex, he was always conscious of his physical shortcomings and Elizabeth's pet names for him – her 'Pygmy' or 'Elf' – showed that she too, even though with sharp but affectionate humour, marked him out from other men. But what he lacked in stature, he made up for in political acumen and intelligence that shone from his delicate, attractive face. He might not have been able to take part in all the sports and forms of hunting that were part of a gentleman's life, but he loved the intricacies and wit of language and poetry. Self-possessed, always cool and calm under pressure, he was the match of anyone at Elizabeth's court.

His father had been at Elizabeth's side since she was first declared Queen at Hatfield in 1558 and had also served under both her brother Edward VI and her sister, Mary. It was a remarkable record for anyone in those turbulent Tudor times, when backing the wrong cause could lead straight to a violent death, but Burghley was not called 'the Fox' for nothing. Elizabeth trusted him to serve the crown, embodied in his Queen, and they made a formidable team. He was her Secretary of State from the beginning and in 1572 was made Lord Treasurer, with Walsingham as Secretary of State. A cultivated man, who set great store by education and the status quo of England's hierarchy, he passed on his vast experience to up-and-coming Robert.

For many years, father and son worked alongside each other. When Walsingham died in 1590, Burghley took over the post of Secretary of State 'temporarily' in addition to his role as Lord Treasurer. Whoever held that position was very close to the Queen – it meant controlling home affairs, foreign affairs and the extensive spy network that stretched throughout Europe. He

ROBERT CECIL (1563–1612)

wanted Robert to take the post, and although as yet his son was too young and inexperienced for such a responsible role he was not about to allow anyone else to appropriate it. So, for the next few years, Robert did the work while his father ostensibly took the responsibility – it was a subterfuge that fooled no one, least of all Elizabeth, but she was happy with the situation and knighted Robert in 1591 after a visit to Theobalds, afterwards appointing him to the Privy Council.

Theobalds (pronounced 'Tibbalds') was Burghley's extravagant, exuberant mansion in Hertfordshire, near Cheshunt, where he often entertained Elizabeth and her court. When Burghley died he left the house to Robert Cecil, who added to its Renaissance fancies. It was said, for instance, to have a hall made to look like a forest, with artificial trees and a 'sky' overhead that held a mechanical sun and stars that could twinkle at night. Sadly, this great house was demolished in 1651.

Robert took advantage of his unique position to learn all he could and to make himself indispensable to the Queen. Things were not going all his way however. Not everyone at court was pleased to see Burghley creating a political dynasty, including two of the most meddlesome and wayward of Elizabeth's courtiers – the young Earl of Essex and Sir Walter Raleigh, aided and abetted by Robert's cousin, Francis Bacon. It was not Robert's way to fall out with anyone at court, but they sorely tried his patience.

Essex was particularly dangerous, since he was the old Queen's favourite, and every time an influential post came up at court he tried to get his man in and keep Cecil's out, mostly unsuccessfully. Elizabeth forgave Essex a lot for his handsome, graceful glamour, but she was never a total fool for love and in the end Essex went too far and plotted against her; he was executed for treason in 1601. At his trial he tried to implicate Cecil, who, in a rare show of emotion, fought back: 'The difference between me and you is great. For wit I give you pre-eminence. For nobility I also give you place. I am no swordsman; there also you have the odds. But,' he went on, 'I have innocence, conscience, truth and honesty to defend me.' Elizabeth never doubted that, just as she had never doubted his father.

Essex had been particularly irritated that in 1596, when he was indulging in one of his greatest flamboyant acts for his Queen, the capture of Cadiz and the Spanish fleet, at home Robert Cecil finally succeeded in being appointed Chief Secretary in his own right. That meant that for a couple of years father and son ran the government and stood together at the Queen's right hand, Burghley died in 1598, leaving his son to carry on alone.

Burghley gave his son three things to aim for in his life's work: to shun war and foreign entanglements, to whenever possible reconcile Elizabeth with her enemies, and to work for a peaceful succession. Cecil believed the last of those three was now the most important. If there was a dispute when Elizabeth died, if the country should be dragged into conflict as it had been in times past, then all that he and his father – and Elizabeth herself – had done to create a wealthy, peaceful and united country would be for nothing. When Burghley died, Elizabeth was in her mid-sixties. No matter how she tried to ignore the fact, her death must now be a factor in any political planning for the new century.

There were three possible claimants for Elizabeth's throne – Lady Arabella Stuart, the Infanta of Castile, and King James VI of Scotland. In Cecil's eyes, there was only one contender: James was the son of Mary, Queen of Scots and like Elizabeth, a direct descendant of Henry VII; the others were mere figureheads for interested parties. As early as 1601, he made contact with James and began the slow and painstaking, and very secret, negotiations that would bring the Scottish King to the English throne.

When, finally, Elizabeth lay on her deathbed she could put off the question no more. Who did she name as her successor? 'I will

ROBERT CECIL (1563–1612)

have no rascal to succeed me; and who should succeed me but a king?' she whispered. Urged to make herself plainer, she confirmed it would be 'our cousin of Scotland'. Shortly afterwards she died, on 24th March 1603, in her 70th year. Cecil was able to proclaim James King of England and the news spread rapidly throughout the kingdom, received quietly and without fuss.

Cecil set off on horseback northwards, to greet his new king. James came from the North to London surrounded by his Scottish followers and England's courtiers flocked to meet him, eager to be among the first to salute their monarch. By the time he got to London, he had already created 300 new knights and the prospect of honours and riches from this newcomer was a sweet temptation for those who had perhaps failed to make their way with their more worldly wise queen.

James was not in Elizabeth's sterling mould, and Cecil must have had his private doubts about the man himself, though never about the honour due to the anointed monarch. He would continue to serve as he had always done, but whether his heart was in it is in doubt. James had been King of Scotland since 1567, but had learned little about good governance. He was an unattractive man, morally suspect and less intellectual than he believed himself to be. His relationship with Cecil was not an easy one and he kept his chief minister at arm's length. It was not a happy time for Cecil, but James did recognise what he owed to his 'Great Little Secretary' – in 1603 he created him Lord Cecil, followed by Viscount Cranborne, and finally Earl of Salisbury in 1605. Two years later he appointed him Lord Treasurer, the first time that one person had officially held the two major posts in English politics.

Despite his years of service Cecil was unpopular with the public, who had often sided with more flamboyant, colourful characters like Essex or Raleigh against him. There was no one to help him shoulder the weight of work that he still carried out. As a young man in his twenties he had been married, happily, to a girl he fell in love with at first sight, but his Elizabeth had died in 1596 after only a few years, leaving him the lone father of one son and two daughters. He loved his children and tried to do his best by them, and his name was linked with many women over the years, including a fair number of married women, but he never remarried.

There was, however, one great interest in which he could indulge himself. Like his father, and many other great noblemen in that age, he had a love of architecture and design – he had already built houses in Chelsea and Cranborne, and Salisbury House on the banks of the Thames. Theobalds was his playground for years, but it was such a wonderful place that it was not long before James was making it plain that he wanted it for himself. In exchange, in 1607 he gave Salisbury properties scattered over England, including the old palace of Hatfield.

Salisbury immediately planned the building of an entirely new mansion, one which would reflect his wealth and status as England's premier politician. Work began in 1607 and took five years and more, costing a small fortune. He built the greatest Jacobean house in Hertfordshire today, its architecture and gardens a delight and a wonder. But he did not live to enjoy it. Robert Cecil, Earl of Salisbury, died on 24th May 1612, on his way home from a visit to Bath which he had hoped would improve his health. He was brought back to Hatfield and buried in the church of St Etheldreda, close by the walls of Hatfield House. The thread that had run through the reign of the Tudors and bound it seamlessly with the Stuart kings was broken.

7

Apsley Cherry-Garrard (1886–1959)

With Scott to the Antarctic

When Captain Robert Falcon Scott – 'Scott of the Antarctic' – returned from his first National Antarctic Expedition in 1904, it was to a world enthralled by the notion of polar exploration. Reports of the vast white lands through which Scott had travelled captured the public imagination, and when he announced that he was going back, to not only undertake scientific studies but also in an endeavour to be the first to reach the South Pole, over 8,000 men applied to go with him. Out of those eager volunteers he handpicked a team that included men whose names have become part of our national folklore – Wilson, Oates, Bowers, Evans. And amongst the party that set off in the *Terra Nova* on 15th June 1910 was a 24-year-old from Hertfordshire – Apsley George Benet Cherry-Garrard, known to all simply as 'Cherry'.

Cherry was a young man looking for a purpose in life. In 1907 he had inherited the Lamer estate at Wheathampstead and other estates in Berkshire and Oxfordshire from his father. Lamer was his home, where he had grown up from the age of six, and he loved it there, but the responsibilities that came with being the head of the family were oppressive and although he had travelled the world he had still not found what he was looking for. In the company of Scott and his fellow explorers, he was entering a time that would be the high spot of his life – after this expedition, which would take him to the extremes of physical and mental endurance, everything else would be anti-climax.

He had been a shy, sensitive boy but he took to the close-knit

Apsley Cherry-Garrard (Herts Advertiser)

world of the polar party with an endearing willingness to learn. Scott wrote of him that 'his whole heart is in the life, with profound eagerness to help everyone'. Always cheerful and hard-working, he proved to be intelligent, practical, resourceful and courageous, qualities essential for the hardships they faced. He did it all, too, under the disadvantage of being as blind as a bat without his glasses.

After the long journey south by sea, Scott's party arrived in New Zealand in October 1910 and a month later sailed for Antarctica, the *Terra Nova* overladen and suffering in the gales and stormy seas. Sailing through the floes of the ice pack was an amazing experience, full of wonder for Cherry. Here he encountered whales, sea-leopards and the Antarctic penguins for the first time. For penguins he had a special affection, 'these little people of the

APSLEY CHERRY-GARRARD (1886–1959)

Antarctic world', even though they were to nearly cost him his life a year later.

The team of explorers reached the Antarctic continent in the polar midsummer, early in 1911, anchoring off Cape Evans, their main land station, where Mounts Erebus and Terror towered above. They now had a limited period before the deep winter nights would set in, so they set about rebuilding the old hut Scott had last seen some years before – this would be 'Hut Point'. Then came their first major expedition, to lay supply depots in preparation for the long journey south to the Pole.

The weather was against them but they headed first for Base Camp, seven miles away, and then another 27 miles on to Corner Camp, where a three-day blizzard kept them pinned down. On 8th February they finally left Corner Camp and eight days later were 144 miles from Cape Evans, at One Ton Camp, where most

The start of Scott's expedition to the Pole, with Cherry-Garrard amongst his companions. (The Sphere)

of the supplies were left. It was an eventful journey, most especially for Cherry when he and Bowers were marooned alone for several hours on an ice floe that had broken free of the pack, surrounded by 'a host of the terrible 'killer' whales'. For a time Scott believed them to be lost forever, but their luck held.

By the time they were all back at Cape Evans it was the end of April and the polar night had set in. They would have a long wait until they could set out for the Pole, in November 1911. By then they knew that the Norwegian explorer, Amundsen, was also poised to be the first to reach the South Pole.

Now came the most terrifying five weeks of Cherry's life. He was on the expedition as assistant zoologist to Edward 'Bill' Wilson, Chief of the Scientific Staff, and Wilson had a desire to travel to the emperor penguin colony known to be at Cape Crozier, beneath Mount Terror. He wanted to bring back eggs, hoping that the developing embryos, when examined in London, would prove the missing link between birds and reptiles. It was a serious scientific aim, but one that put enormous strain on the three men who went on the Winter Journey – Wilson, Bowers and Cherry.

Leaving Cape Evans behind, it took them nineteen days to reach Cape Crozier – days when for the most part they were travelling in darkness, hauling the sledges themselves and sometimes going as little as a mile or two at a time. Their sweat froze, so that ice formed on their bodies; once Cherry's clothes froze on him within fifteen seconds of leaving the tent, encasing him in an armour of ice. They contended with snow, wind and fog, their hands and feet were blistered and frostbite set in, and the temperature at one point reached minus 77 degrees. When finally they reached Cape Crozier, they were stopped in their tracks by a blizzard that lasted three days.

They pitched their camp 800 ft up on the mountainside. The views were magnificent, but Cherry's reaction showed their exhaustion: 'Oh God, what a place!' They had to descend the ice cliffs to get to the penguin colony, the first men to ever set foot there, and were able to collect five eggs before they were forced away by the huge birds. On the way back, Cherry broke the two eggs he was carrying.

Before they could start back, a blizzard of titanic proportions set in. It blew away their tent and they had to resort to the igloo they had built for their stores. There they lay, listening to the howling hurricane battering at the ice blocks around them, and began to contemplate death. At last, the wind dropped and they could set out on the return journey. They walked in the dark, covered in ice, ravenously hungry and so exhausted that they almost slept as they walked. No words could express the horror of that journey, Cherry said later. And then they were there, opening the door of the hut at Cape Evans and in effect coming back from the dead. Scott called their expedition 'one of the most gallant stories in Polar History'. Sadly, those three penguin eggs would not provide the scientific breakthrough that Wilson had hoped for.

Three months later, it was time to begin the march south. On 1st November 1911, Scott set out with a party that included Cherry, but Cherry would not be going to the Pole. Only five men would be in the final team and he was one of those sent back to Cape Evans on 22nd December. Only Scott, Bowers, Oates, Evans and Wilson made the final journey.

During March, Cherry and his companions visited One Ton and Hut Point, making sure all was in order for Scott's return. At first unconcerned, by the end of the month they were beginning to fear the worst and the certainty that the polar party were dead was acknowledged by May. At last spring arrived and at the end of October a search party set out from Hut Point. They found Scott on 12th November, only eleven miles from One Ton, dead in the tent with Bowers and Wilson. Oates' body was discovered a little later, where he had walked out into the snow rather than be a burden to his comrades. Evans had died earlier on that last terrible journey. They had been beaten to the South Pole by Amundsen by as little as a month.

The whole story of Scott's expedition and death has passed into legend – the news was greeted with shock at home in England and the men who had failed to reach the Pole were elevated to heroes by the manner of their failure. It was Cherry who suggested the lines of Tennyson's *Ulysses* that the men of the expedition inscribed on the cross they raised to their lost comrades at Observation Point: *To strive, to seek, to find, and not to yield.*

Cherry returned home to Lamer, but he never again found that elusive spirit that had elevated the men who went with Scott to almost superhuman endurance and character. In 1914 when the First World War broke out he volunteered as a dispatch rider and joined the 8th Signalling Company, Royal Engineers, later being transferred to armoured cars as a Lieutenant Commander RNVR. He served in Flanders during 1915, but his health was poor and he was invalided out. Back home again at Lamer, he began to write *The Worst Journey in the World*, his enthralling account of Scott's expedition, which he finished in 1922. Amongst his closest friends were George Bernard Shaw and his wife, living at nearby Ayot St Lawrence, and he often said that Shaw had shown him how to write.

Certain subjects interested him for the rest of his life, including exploration and wildlife. In 1916, for instance, he took up the case of the king penguins on Macquarie Island, which were being cruelly killed for their oil and was successful in persuading the Tasmanian government to ban the hunting and make the island a wildlife sanctuary. About 20 years later, he showed compassion for the hunted again when he brought an action against the local fox-hunt for trespass and damage on his Wheathampstead estate.

He married Angela Turner in 1939, but even his happiness with her could not disguise the increasing depression he felt. The war did not help, and in 1947 he was forced to leave Lamer, unable to keep up such a large mansion any longer. He moved to a London flat, in Gloucester Place, and spent much of his time brooding about whether he could have saved Scott and the others – if only he had gone on to look for them when he was at One Ton in March that year, if only ...

The regret and self-recrimination Cherry felt later in his life could not be argued away by his many friends, though no one could ever say for sure whether any action of his would have made the slightest bit of difference to Scott's fate. For a time he enjoyed good health, but he broke down again in 1953 and died on 18th May 1959, aged 75.

Cherry was buried in the family vault at Wheathampstead church, and three years later a memorial statue of a man in polar dress, by the sculptor Ivor Roberts-Jones, was placed in the church, where it remains today.

8

Sir Geoffrey de Havilland (1882–1965)

Aeronautical pioneer

On 20th September 1941, during the Second World War, four small aircraft were sent out from England on a photographic reconnaissance sortie over Bordeaux in occupied France. As soon as they were detected, the Luftwaffe sent up its own Messerschmitt 109s to intercept. But to the surprise of the German pilots, they could not match the speed of the British planes and all returned safely to England. The Mosquito, conceived, designed and built by Geoffrey de Havilland in Hertfordshire, had made its wartime debut.

The 'Mossie' became a favourite of RAF pilots, in its many forms. It could fly at some twenty miles an hour faster than a Spitfire, which might mean the difference between life and death, and it could be adapted to a wide range of roles, whether photo-reconnaissance, night-fighter, day-fighter, fighter-bomber, bomber, anti-shipping striker, or pathfinder.

Men flying Mosquitoes discovered the 'V' weapon sites at Peenemunde, bombed U-boats, defended the coasts of England against the Luftwaffe, and undertook pinpoint bombing raids over continental targets. In July 1942 on a photo-reconnaissance flight seeking the German battleship *Tirpitz*, a Mosquito was flown 3,000 miles in a day, on a round trip that took in Narvik in Scandinavia, and Murmansk in Russia, and this was not an isolated occurrence. Air Chief Marshal Sir Basil Embry said that, 'In my opinion the Mosquito is the finest aeroplane, without exception, that has ever been built in this country.'

Its creator, he could have added, was one of the finest

SIR GEOFFREY DE HAVILLAND (1882–1965)

aeroplane designers and builders in this country, if not the world, and there was a great deal more to him than just the Mosquito. His name has become synonymous with Hatfield, where his company was the major employer in civil and military aviation over several decades and where he is not forgotten today.

Geoffrey de Havilland was born on 27th July 1882 at Haslemere in Surrey, the son of a clergyman. A fascination with engineering that began with the design of cars and motorbikes crystallised into a lifelong love of aviation after Wilbur Wright demonstrated his new flying machine at Le Mans in 1908. He didn't actually see Wright fly, and had only had one short glimpse of a plane in the air, but inspired and undaunted he nonetheless

Geoffrey de Havilland. (de Havilland Aircraft Heritage Centre)

set about designing and building his own biplane, which flew on the second attempt on 10th September 1910.

'Number Two' was sold to the War Office and Geoffrey was offered a job in the Army's Farnborough Balloon Factory, where they were experimenting with the new machines. He was still there when war was declared in August 1914, and spent most of the war working at Airco on designs for the new Royal Flying Corps.

One day when flying, Geoffrey had been able to get above the clouds and he never forgot the experience. He found himself in 'a blinding world of billowing whiteness . . . magnificent, vast and thrilling'. His enjoyment never faded and he flew whenever he could. He married Louie Thomas in 1909 and luckily she enjoyed flying as much as he did. He had taken her up in 'Number Two' in the early days – holding his eight-week-old baby son, Geoffrey! They flew together all over England and the Continent, and even over Africa on safari, though Louie admitted that she preferred the enclosed cockpits of later years.

When the war ended Geoffrey was financially secure from the royalties paid by the government for the planes he had designed. With the aid of a substantial loan from George Holt Thomas, the founder of Airco, he decided to go into business for himself and set up the de Havilland Aircraft Company, concentrating on civil aircraft. The company was registered on 25th September 1920 and began life on the old aerodrome at Stag Lane, Edgware.

In those inter-war years private flying really, if you'll pardon the pun, took off and the company were soon producing not only aircraft for civil airlines, but also small craft for single pilots. In fact, de Havilland helped to create a market, making planes accessible to those who were becoming enthralled by the idea of flight, perhaps by going to see Alan Cobham's Flying Circus that toured the country in the early 1930s and performed at Royston, Hitchin, Elstree and Hertford.

SIR GEOFFREY DE HAVILLAND (1882–1965)

De Havilland came to Hatfield in 1932, when the Stag Lane premises became too enclosed by new suburban housing for safety. At Hatfield, he purchased the surrounding farmland to prevent the same problem arising for his new site.

The great success of the early years was the Moth type aircraft, the Tiger Moth and Gypsy Moth being perhaps the most widely known specimens but only two of many, such as the Cirrus Moth, the Hornet Moth, the Puss Moth, the Leopard Moth, the Fox Moth and so on. By 1929, three Gypsy Moths were being built every day, as well as those on licence in America and France. Many airmen will remember training in the Tiger Moth, which was designed especially for the RAF.

Hatfield became a busy airfield, popular with fliers and the scene of many triumphs for the de Havilland Company. Just a year after settling in, the prestigious King's Cup air race was based there – and won by Geoffrey de Havilland in his Leopard Moth – and in 1934 the first Empire Air Day opened the aerodrome to the public. Local people became used to seeing unusual aircraft flying low overhead, sometimes on test flights, sometimes just visiting, and were proud of the success and prestige of their neighbour.

Geoffrey de Havilland created not only a world-renowned technically successful operation, but also one which reflected his care and concern for the people who worked for him, from those in the offices to those on the workshop floor. To a great extent, de Havilland became Hatfield, so many of the local people worked there, father and son, mother and daughter. Apprenticeships at the factory were eagerly snapped up and would give any trainee the prospect of certain work in any branch of engineering, so good was the quality of training. Many, though, never left de Havilland, preferring to remain with the company throughout their working life and keeping up links with fellow workers long after retirement. When a new plane went out on its first test flight, the whole company felt that they had had some part in putting it together.

The Mosquito was part of the family. Geoffrey de Havilland, like so many others of his generation, had realised by the late 1930s that war was looming once again and he had it in mind to design a high-speed unarmed bomber, built of wood – metal might be in short supply in wartime, he reasoned, but wood was likely to be abundant. He found little support from the Air Ministry at first but research and design went on with urgency after war was declared in 1939 and the first order came through for 50 of these 'wooden wonders' in March 1940. The prototype was actually built at Salisbury Hall, near London Colney, where secrecy could be maintained, and then flown from Hatfield on 25th November 1940.

The Mosquito dominated wartime de Havilland, and demand was so great that some had to be made at Leavesden, near Watford, as well as at other plants around the country and under licence in Canada and Australia. Almost 8,000 were built. The work being done at Hatfield made it a prime target for Luftwaffe bombers and on 3rd October 1940, 21 workers died and over 70 were injured in a bombing raid. The last Hatfield-built Mosquito was completed in April 1946, though it still flew with the RAF until 1955. It was the fastest aircraft in the world from September 1941 to early 1944, and had been diversified into 40 variants.

The test pilot on that first flight in 1940 was Geoffrey de Havilland junior. Several members of the de Havilland family worked with the company, including Geoffrey junior and John, two of Geoffrey's sons, as test pilots. Their father recounted the story of how, when Geoffrey and Peter (his middle son) were six and three years old respectively, he had taken them up in a plane to introduce them to flying. The pair were unimpressed: 'Peter took no notice at all except to spit over the side "to see where it would go". . . while Geoffrey, whose passion at the time was for

SIR GEOFFREY DE HAVILLAND (1882–1965)

A Mosquito at the de Havilland airfield at Hatfield. (Ian Simpson)

trains, kept his eye on the railway line to see where it went.' Any fatherly disappointment was later assuaged by their own passion for the air.

This was, however, to lead to tragedy for the family. John was killed on a Mosquito test flight in 1944, and Geoffrey junior was killed on 27th September 1946. He had gone up in a DH 108, a small jet-engined aircraft, from Hatfield to make a final test before attempting the world speed record, but the plane 'exploded' over the Thames Estuary; his body was not found for several days. This second death proved too much for their mother, Louie, and she too died not long after. They were all buried in the churchyard at Tewin, where they had lived for a period during the war. The losses were deeply felt at Hatfield, by the entire workforce.

Aircraft enthusiasts will know that a list of the innovations and aircraft, military and civil, developed by de Havilland both before and after the war would be long and varied. It included, for instance, Britain's first jet fighter, the Goblin-powered Gloster Meteor, the Sprite rocket engine, the Vampire jet that was the first aircraft to exceed 500 mph, the Firestreak guided weapon – the range is far too extensive for this brief chapter to pay tribute to them all. To pick out just one more story – on 2nd May 1952, the Comet airliner, the first to be powered by four turbojet engines, began passenger services between London and Johannesburg for the British Overseas Airways Corporation (BOAC). No other airliner had anything like it, and it had been designed and built 'off the drawing board' at Hatfield.

The Comet caught the popular imagination all round the world, but it then had to overcome a terrible start to its service life when fatal accidents involving the aircraft took place in 1954, with the loss of 56 lives. The shock and numb horror felt at Hatfield gave way to a determination to put things right and it was discovered that a weakness in the cabin structure had caused the aircraft to disintegrate in flight. The problems of metal fatigue had not then been fully realised, as was made clear at the Court of Inquiry in 1954. The Comet did fly again, but only after a huge commitment to research and testing by the de Havilland workforce.

It was typical of Sir Geoffrey de Havilland's care for his company as a whole that in his autobiography *Sky Fever*, when discussing the failure of the Comet, he paid tribute to the 'staff responsible for finance, business, sales and factory organisation' for their work in keeping things going while the Comet was redesigned and rebuilt. It was that concern and gratitude for the work of even the smallest cog in the company wheel that made him such an exemplary employer. Relationships between workers and management were always good and in no small part was this due to the personality of the boss, who 'always found it natural

SIR GEOFFREY DE HAVILLAND (1882–1965)

to meet people on equal terms and treat them, and be treated, with complete freedom and sincerity'.

In 1960 the de Havilland Group was taken over by Hawker Siddeley, and in due course that name too would disappear and be replaced by British Aerospace. Manufacturing ceased on the Hatfield site in 1993, and today you will find it largely built over by a business park, housing and the University of Hertfordshire. There are reminders of the old days in the names of the streets and of course, in the long-established Comet hotel nearby. The story of de Havilland, and the Mosquito, is however enthusiastically commemorated at the de Havilland Aircraft Heritage Centre at Salisbury Hall, London Colney, where the prototype Mosquito and other de Havilland planes can be seen.

Sir Geoffrey de Havilland was a man of great vision and determination, but unlike some others of that ilk, he was also a good man in the world outside his work. He was honoured several times – including an OBE in 1918, the Air Force Cross in 1919, a CBE in 1934, a knighthood in 1944 and the Order of Merit in 1962. He wrote his autobiography in his eighties, when he could look back on a life that spanned the history of manned flight, from those first bumpy hops into the air to the development of the space rocket. By that time he had reluctantly retired from active participation in the company but was still going regularly to Hatfield as President. Happily, after the terrible shock of losing three members of his family in a few short years, he had married again, to Joan Mordaunt.

He died on 21st May 1965, at Watford Peace Memorial Hospital. After the funeral, his ashes were taken by plane over Seven Barrows in Hampshire and scattered there, where he had first taken to the air.

◆

9

Thomas Dimsdale (1712–1800)

The doctor who saved Catherine the Great from smallpox

The 'small pox' was one of the handful of diseases that have been proved to have affected the course of human history. So called to differentiate it from the 'great pox' (syphilis), in the 18th century it was widespread and dangerous, and could be hideously disfiguring. The sufferer would be suddenly struck down with a high fever and crippling muscular pain. After two to five days of this, if not already dead of internal haemorrhage, he or she would be covered by a rash of pimples, which rapidly became large pustules. Secondary infection while the skin was raw led to more deaths. Many survived, but were scarred for life. The author Herman Melville described the effect of smallpox on the skin as being 'like the complicated ribbed bed of a torrent, when the rushing waters have been dried up'.

Smallpox could be caught by coming into contact with the pus or scabs of a victim, or more commonly by inhaling the virus from their breath. It spread rapidly in any community, and could be caught by rich and poor alike. Is it any wonder that a physician who could claim to protect against catching the disease would be sought after? Though perhaps a request that he travel 2,000 miles from his native Hertfordshire to inoculate the Empress of Russia was out of the ordinary!

Thomas Dimsdale was born on 29th May 1712, the fourth son of Sir John and Susanna Dimsdale, at Theydon Garnon in Essex. The family were Quakers with a strong interest in medicine. Sir John had travelled to New England in America with William Penn in 1684 as medical adviser, though he had decided to return home a few years later, while the Hertford branch of the Dimsdale family ran a medical practice with a wide catchment area. When he was only fourteen years old, Thomas inherited property from that Hertford branch that made him overnight a man of means, who could afford to choose his own path in life. The overriding influences in that life were to be his strong Quaker faith, his interest in medicine, his taste for travel, and an adventuring spirit.

In the 1730s, after studying at St Thomas's Hospital in London, Thomas took up the Hertford practice. The death of his first wife, Mary, unsettled him for a time and he went off to be a volunteer surgeon with the army that faced the followers of Bonnie Prince Charlie in 1745, but he was soon back in Hertford, though he did not go back to doctoring until 1761. In the meantime he married again, to Ann Iles, and this was to be a long and happy relationship that brought him ten children.

Dr Thomas Dimsdale.

Now he seems to have decided to do things properly. He had never actually gained a qualification from St Thomas's Hospital, so he went back to his studies, this time at King's College in Aberdeen, and graduated as a physician. Back home, he bought Port Hill House, between Hertford and Bengeo, and opened a 'pest house' where he could follow his interest in the treatment and prevention of smallpox. And in 1767 he published *The Present Method of Inoculating for the Small Pox*, which sold in seven editions and was translated into several languages.

Thomas's method of inoculating was known as 'variolation'. It meant to vaccinate by introducing a mild form of the virus into the body, because surviving the disease gave immunity for life. It was an old idea, and Thomas was by no means the only doctor using this method, but he had devised his own regime of care and 'secret' medicine to augment the actual introduction of the infection into a patient via a small incision in their flesh. It seemed to have caught the public imagination, at any rate.

There was no intention to use the method to make himself rich. He was in any event already quite well off, and his care was often for the poor. In January 1768 he was called in to see a young boy named George Hodges, aged ten, at Little Berkhamsted. The lad was very ill with smallpox and Thomas could do little for him at that stage of the disease, apart from easing his suffering as best he could. The Revd. Richard Levett recalled that Thomas 'with a humanity peculiar to himself, washed him, removed all nasty obstructions and by his care, preserved his life some days'. The boy died, and now Thomas's care was for the living. He knew he could do something to stop the disease spreading, so he offered to inoculate everyone in the parish free of charge. The plan was so successful that neighbouring Bayford asked if he would do the same for them, which he gladly did.

That same year, just a few months after little George's death, a strange and exotic visitor arrived at Thomas's home. The Russian

THOMAS DIMSDALE (1712–1800)

Ambassador had come with an invitation to travel to St Petersburg, to the court of Catherine the Great, to inoculate the Empress and her son and heir, the Grand Duke.

Why Catherine chose this country doctor from Hertfordshire is not known for certain. It may have had something to do with reports from Dr Jan Ingenhouz, a Dutch doctor who had been staying with Thomas to observe his methods during the Little Berkhamsted episode – he was now physician to the Empress Maria Theresa of Austria and successfully inoculated three of her children. Maria Theresa's experience the year before was certainly known to Catherine – smallpox had ravaged the imperial Hapsburg family, killing the Empress's daughter and daughter-in-law and scarring the Empress herself and two other daughters.

Catherine was determined to have Thomas Dimsdale, and have him she did. At the end of July 1768, he and his son Nathaniel, a 20-year-old medical student, set off from Hertford on the long journey to Russia. He must have known, with some trepidation, that this was no ordinary journey. He would be welcomed by few in Russia apart from Catherine herself, and the hostility of the Russian 'old guard' was enough to give anyone pause. Neither nobles nor the Church wanted Western medicine imposed on them. And the British government weren't too keen on the idea either – inoculation was a risky business and Thomas's failure could reflect back on Britain itself and affect our ambitions in the rich Russian trading areas. Thomas would be walking a knife-edge. Any blunder, and it was doubtful he would leave Russia alive. It was said that he only agreed to go if Catherine personally ensured that there was an escape route for him and his son if anything went wrong.

Thomas and Nathaniel arrived in St Petersburg at the end of August 1768, after a month of hard travelling by day and night. Thomas was no youngster, but even at 56 he seems to have arrived quite fresh, which says much for his stamina and good health.

Thomas was impressed by the glittering Russian court – though he realised at once that he would have to watch his step with some of the people he met. Catherine was a passionate, energetic, cunning, stubborn woman who was absolute ruler of one of the most magnificent, wealthy, backward, savage countries in the world. She had deposed her own husband, Peter III, in 1762 and ascended the throne as Catherine II, by which time Peter had been murdered by her lover. She would spend the next 34 years trying to make Russia a place of culture and enlightenment and to extend its empire. It is to her credit that she did not use force or terror, preferring to persuade by reforms and legislation, but she had her vices and became more autocratic as she aged.

Despite Thomas's misgivings, Catherine insisted on keeping her plans a secret ('a secret which everybody knows', reported the English Ambassador). On 12th October 1768 a coach took Thomas to the palace, and that evening he inoculated the Empress with smallpox. A small boy named Alexander Markov provided the infected matter that was placed within the small incision made in her skin. Afterwards Thomas went back to his lodgings. His feelings that night can be imagined.

Catherine went to her country palace, Tsarskoe Selo, where she could be isolated, and Thomas followed her there. To his relief, everything went very well and apart from some discomfort Catherine's brush with smallpox was mild. She returned to St Petersburg on 1st November, completely healthy and now immune to smallpox, and the next day her son, the Grand Duke, was inoculated, again without problems. National holidays were declared in thanksgiving.

A load was lifted from Thomas and Nathaniel's shoulders. Compliments poured in from the hitherto suspicious nobles and churchmen, and he could soon add 140 noblemen and an archbishop to his tally of those successfully inoculated. By 1772 clinics had been set up in cities all over Russia, even as far away as Irkutsk in Siberia. Some 20,000 Russians are said to have been inoculated by 1780, and a million by 1800.

Thomas was richly rewarded for his work. Catherine gave him £12,000 and an annuity of £500 for life, as well as making him a Councillor of State. He and his son were created Barons of the Russian Empire, and his family coat of arms was allowed to be emblazoned with the black wing of the Imperial Russian eagle, in a gold shield. Thomas's son, John, received Royal licence in 1813 to use the title in this country.

Thomas and Nathaniel had to wait out the Russian winter before they could start for home, and set off in early spring 1769. Thomas would return twelve years later to inoculate Catherine's grandsons.

Back home in Hertford, he found himself a celebrity. He was pleased to be elected a Fellow of the Royal Society, but continued his work locally. Ann's death in 1779 was a heavy blow, but he remarried quickly, to Elizabeth Dimsdale, a distant relative (who went to Russia with him in 1781), and retained his interest in life. He even served as Hertford's Member of Parliament for over ten years until 1790, when he was 78. He spent the last years of his life at Essendon, and died in 1800, aged 88. He chose to be buried in the Quaker burial ground at Bishop's Stortford on the border of the county with Essex, where other members of his family lived.

Thomas lived just long enough to see his method of inoculation overtaken by a new discovery that would eventually rid the world of this ancient scourge. Edward Jenner, a physician from Gloucestershire, had realised that some of his patients who had already suffered from cowpox – a mild disease caught from livestock – did not develop smallpox when inoculated. In other words, they seemed to have developed immunity to the more deadly disease. He tested the theory on others, including his own son, before publishing his results in 1798; he called his new method 'vaccination'. Within a century, death from smallpox in England was practically unknown, and by the late 20th century the disease was officially extinct in the world. The result would have delighted Thomas.

10

John M. East (1860–1924)

Pioneer of 'the British Hollywood'

Strange to think on what an element of chance some great things rest. It was, for instance, pure chance that one Sunday afternoon in 1913, two brothers were motoring on a quest through the southern stretches of the county when, in the tiny hamlet of Boreham Wood, in Elstree parish, they came across the combination of circumstances that answered their needs perfectly. Clear, clean air; beautiful countryside; a railway station that promised easy access to central London; and, strangest of all, a sale board conveniently advertising that seven acres of land were available immediately.

The first two they could have found at most places in Hertfordshire, the third was not so strange in this county; but to get all that and a plot of land was pure serendipity. From that afternoon drive grew, slowly and not without setbacks, one of the major sites of British cinema and television production, known almost at once as 'the British Hollywood'. One of the men in the car was John M. East, actor, manager, producer, and film pioneer.

East had begun his career in the 1880s as a stage actor, and then added theatre management to his achievements; at one time he managed the Lyric in Hammersmith, and several other London theatres, and arranged stage tours around the country. The stage, however, could not contain his dramatic vision. In 1909 he had put on a show at the Crystal Palace called *Invasion*, in which he dramatised the possibility of bombardment by enemy airship – a few years before the real thing happened (see Chapter 16). He used 600 actors and apparently was frighteningly convincing – it

John M. East, pioneer film producer at Elstree.

was a technique that would be familiar to every director of disaster movies since then. He was very interested in the potential of film to burst out of the restriction of stage action and became convinced that he could make a successful business out of film production.

By 1913 the film industry was firmly established both here and abroad and it has been estimated that there were about 600 cinemas in operation by that time in Greater London alone – Elstree had one, a converted chapel in Gasworks Lane. East was by then working as an actor and casting manager for London

JOHN M. EAST (1860–1924)

Films at Twickenham Studios, but he and his friend Percy Nash decided to throw in their lot together and create their own company. They had the support of an influential businessman, Arthur Moss Lawrence, who arranged financial backing and with £40,000 they formed the Neptune Film Company Ltd in January 1914. The site for their new venture would be Boreham Wood, then, and now, known more widely as 'Elstree'.

It was an exciting time to be in the business, then just beginning to find its feet in England as a commercial concern. There were plenty of people experimenting with film, but East was one of those who had the buccaneering spirit that was necessary to drive it as a business. He believed that he could make films that would rival those coming out of Hollywood and he set about creating the most up-to-date studios in Europe to do so.

The purpose-built studios that went up on the plot of land in Clarendon Road, Boreham Wood, contained offices, dressing rooms with all mod cons, a projection theatre, editing rooms, processing laboratories, and all that a modern studio could possibly require. The studio itself was huge for its time, over 70 feet in length, and could be divided up into smaller sets, each with their own solid backdrop, so that several films could be made at the same time – these were still silent films, so background noise was no problem.

But what was unique at that time was that the studio did not need natural light. Every other film studio in England was using premises that, usually, had started life as something completely different – a chapel, perhaps – and every other studio relied for filming on natural light through glass roofs or walls. Neptune's cameraman, Alfonso Frenguelli, created the first 'dark stage', dependent instead purely on artificial light and therefore available for work at any time of day or night, or whatever the weather was doing – a definite improvement in England's climate. There was no electricity laid on, so East used a gas generator to power the lights, some on stands and others suspended from the ceiling of the studio but all moveable and versatile. England's unsophisticated studios, light years behind the Americans, were being shown the way forward at last.

Not that everything was filmed there. East was keen to use the potential of location work, seeing that the future lay in the way film could move between indoor and outdoor action in a way impossible for stage plays to achieve, and camera units – and actors – were soon working in places as far apart as the Scilly Isles and Scotland. East had bought Ivy Lodge, a large house in Theobald Street, for his family and he used that too, for interior shots and for any action that could be set amongst the trees and bushes in the garden. It wouldn't be unusual to see some of the East family furniture being trundled down the road on its way from Theobald Street to Clarendon Road for a particular set. As the song says, anything goes.

East himself appeared in many of his films as a character actor, and also worked as script editor with a man named Brian Daly. This was conveyor-belt work – it had to be to produce enough films to make a profit – and the pressure was on all of them. Days started at 7 am and often went on long into the night – no problem when all they needed was artificial light. A story is told that once East locked Daly in an attic at Ivy Lodge and refused to let him out until he had completed the piece of script needed, kindly furnishing him with writing materials, drinking and washing water, a few apples, and a chamber pot. Daly got out of the window, shinned down the drainpipe and was not seen again till three days later, slightly the worse for wear.

East and Daly adapted and rewrote stage plays and other literary works, as well as creating some original work, to produce the dramas, comedies, thrillers and documentaries that came out of Neptune Films over the next few years. He was quick to see the benefit in having control of other men's work and the

JOHN M. EAST (1860-1924)

company bought the rights to the stage plays of George R. Sims, a popular Victorian writer whose melodramas were reworked and redramatised for film. In fact, their first major feature film was one of Sims', *The Harbour Lights*, which had first seen the light of day in 1885. Audiences liked familiar treats.

Neptune also bought the rights to the works of J.M. Barrie, author of *Peter Pan*, and made *The Little Minister* on location in Scotland, to great critical acclaim. Barrie even wrote a short original piece especially for them, part of which was filmed in the Savoy Hotel in London. They had no difficulty in getting well-known actors, politicians and other celebrities to appear as 'extras', including George Bernard Shaw and the writer G.K. Chesterton – the former appeared dressed as a cowboy in one scene, while the latter consented to be rolled down a hill in a barrel!

East, of course, appeared in the films, and he had a troupe of regular actors and actresses who dashed from one film to another on the huge set. He offered jobs as 'upper class' extras to actors in West End theatres and paid them twelve shillings a day, more if they brought their own costume – which was why up and coming stars like Jack Buchanan could be found smuggling a dress suit out of the stage door after a performance. Local people were also used in some films: the Revd S. Pendred, who ran the school attended by East's two daughters, was a regular extra, as was the taxi driver with the unlikely name of Herr Von Bricke.

Neptune had another claim to fame in those days, as it produced the first English commercial animated cartoon films, drawn by a well-known book illustrator named Lancelot Speed. His 'Bully Boy' series was created to reflect aspects of life on the Western Front, for Neptune, of course, was formed just as the First World War was about to break out.

Although East's output ran mainly to home-grown and often Victorian drama or comedy, the company did produce some war-related films, such as *A Widow's Son*, about a young soldier who won the Victoria Cross, and *His Just Deserts* which naturally featured a spy who got what was coming to him. They also made recruiting films for the government, such as *Women in Munitions*, and *The Royal Naval Division at Work and Play*, the latter featuring Ivor Novello. But it was the war which brought Neptune to an untimely end.

There could not really have been a worse time to try to establish a new entertainment industry. Actors and technicians were called up, some never to return, and a shortage of gas affected the production of electricity, which in turn reduced the time during which the new sets could be used. Even animal films faced difficulties and one film had to be abandoned when the Army requisitioned and removed all the horses, to be sent to the Front. The Entertainments Tax was another nail in the coffin, putting up prices at the cinemas and cutting audience figures and profits.

Film studios all over England were suffering the same problems, made worse by those perennial bugbears of the British film industry – under-investment and American domination. By that time Hollywood was producing films such as D.W. Griffiths' epic *Birth of a Nation*, as well as the universally popular comedies featuring the silent screen greats such as Charlie Chaplin and Buster Keaton. Hollywood had gloss, glamour and money – our own offerings were provincial and unsophisticated by comparison.

With anger, frustration and sadness, East's company ceased production in 1917 and the Neptune Film Company was liquidated in 1921. East sold Ivy Lodge and moved away, returning to acting, but he survived Neptune by only three years. Ivy Lodge was pulled down in the 1920s. The studios in Clarendon Road were leased out and then in a few years taken over by another film company.

It might seem at this point to be the story of a failure, but John

JOHN M. EAST (1860–1924)

M. East had sown an acorn in Boreham Wood that would soon grow into an impressive oak. His vision in creating state-of-the-art studios in this otherwise undistinguished hamlet was justified when, less than ten years later, the Elstree film business was back on an even keel and embracing the new technology of the 'talking pictures'. Alfred Hitchcock, then a young up-and-coming director, made the first British talkie at Elstree – *Blackmail*.

By the 1930s Elstree was at the forefront of the British film industry and international stars such as Errol Flynn, Gregory Peck, Cary Grant, Elizabeth Taylor, John Mills, Alec Guinness and many more were familiar visitors over the next few decades to the studios based here, which included ABPC, MGM and ATV television; musicals, dramas, comedies, thrillers, they were all made here – even blockbusters like the Steven Spielberg *Indiana Jones* films, and the *Star Wars* series. Today the BBC television studios occupy the old Neptune site in Clarendon Road, where the BBC Newsroom South East is based and *Eastenders* has a permanent set, and Boreham Wood continues to be the base for an impressive array of film and television credits. And all because John M. East happened to drive by, one Sunday afternoon in 1913.

———◆———

11

Graham Hill (1929–1975)

World champion racing driver

Thick fog blanketed southern England and the English Channel on the night of 29th November 1975. Visibility was abysmal and the little Piper Aztec plane that took off from Marseilles for the short journey across the Channel to Elstree aerodrome was soon lost to sight in the clouds.

It was not long before fears for the safety of those on board the plane, which seemed to have completely disappeared, were being expressed on the English television news. Then calls began to come in to the emergency services in Barnet. A light aircraft had clipped the tops of trees on Arkley golf course and crashed, bursting into flames as it hit the ground.

Ambulances and fire engines called onto the golf course moved as fast as they could, trying to avoid the dips in the ground and bunkers that hampered them, but nothing could have helped the occupants of the plane. 'There wasn't anything we could do,' Barnet fireman Barry Wilcox told reporters, 'the plane had been on the ground for 20 minutes or more. The only recognisable piece of the plane was the undercarriage and the engines. There had been a big fire.' All six on board were killed, including the pilot – Graham Hill, one of the most charismatic and successful drivers in British motor racing history.

There was some irony in the fact that Hill died in a plane accident, when he had survived over 20 years' participation in a sport where danger and sudden death were ever-present companions. Smoothly good-looking, charming, self-assured, and totally professional, Hill had been the great survivor, at home

GRAHAM HILL (1929–1975)

Graham Hill.

in both the cockpit of a Formula One racing car and the glamorous show business world that took him in as one of their own.

Norman Graham Hill was born on 15th February 1929, and grew up in his Hendon home a boy with an aptitude for mechanical things. An apprenticeship to Smith's Instruments, and a spell of National Service in the Navy, brought no inkling of his future career. Then a magazine advertisement in 1953 changed his life. He paid £1 to drive a racing car for four laps of Brands Hatch, and was hooked. He only went out of curiosity, but he came away determined to be a racing driver.

He left the safe world of Smith's Instruments and hung around in the pits at race tracks, working on cars free for the chance to occasionally drive one – his first race was in 1954, his first win in 1956. At one meeting he met Colin Chapman, and soon went to work as a mechanic at Chapman's Lotus Car works in Hornsey. He never stopped pushing for the chance to drive, though, and in 1957 was finally signed up for Team Lotus. Shortly after, he drove in his first Formula One Grand Prix, at Monaco.

After driving, Hill's other great love was rowing, which was how he met his wife, Bette. They married in 1955 and she was a constant support to him for the rest of his life. Rowing, by the way, was also responsible for the unusual blue and white design of his racing helmet (and also later of his son's, Damon) – it was borrowed from the London Rowing Club, of which he was a member.

Hill had developed his own driving technique, which could be roughly translated as 'take the car by the scruff of its neck', and he began to win races more regularly. Although he officially drove for Team Lotus, he would in fact drive any car that was offered, never going to a racetrack merely to spectate. It could not have been more different from the Formula One racing world of today – a driver like Graham Hill would pride himself on being able to get behind the wheel of any car and make it perform.

In 1959 Lotus relocated to Cheshunt in Hertfordshire, but Hill stayed with them for only a few more months (though he went back to them in 1967). In 1960 he transferred to British Racing Motors (BRM) and began his rise to stardom. He won his first Grand Prix two years later, at Zandvoort – the first British driver to do so in an all-British car – and went on to be proclaimed

GRAHAM HILL (1929–1975)

World Champion. A total of 14 Grand Prix victories would now be chalked up between 1962 and 1969.

Hill was no angel and there were stories of his irritability and aloofness, but one incident is worth repeating, from 1966. It was the Belgian Grand Prix at Spa, the cars skidding around in driving rain, when Jackie Stewart's BRM shot off the road and landed in a farmyard below the raised track. Graham Hill saw the wreck, stopped his car and went down, to find Stewart trapped in the cockpit and covered in petrol, which was burning his skin. With the help of another crashed driver, Bob Bondurant, Hill took over twenty minutes to extricate Stewart, while they waited for officials and the ambulance to arrive. Jackie Stewart said afterwards, 'A lot of other people would have got on with the race. But he was a teammate, he was a friend – absolutely always a gentleman.' Needless to say, they both went on to drive against each other with great rivalry!

That year, MGM film crews were at several Grand Prix circuits filming for *Grand Prix*, starring James Garner. Hill even had a part in the film, as 'Bob Turner', a racing driver of course. Show business and motor racing had fallen in love with each other, and the general public had fallen in love with Graham Hill, a very British hero. He was made for this role, happy to make speeches and public appearances, to attend film premieres and parties with the other beautiful people, or to entertain a television audience. He seemed to be in the newspapers as often for his social life as for his driving appearances.

The legend was enhanced when he took part in, and won, the Indianapolis 500 race in May 1966. Some writers have described the race as 'confused', and certainly a start that ended in the worst pile-up ever seen at Indianapolis cannot have been the greatest welcome to a rookie driver. However, nothing daunted Graham Hill – he was only the second driver to have won the Indie 'first time', and the first had done so 40 years previously.

If 1966 had been a good year, then so was 1968. Hill won the World Championship for the second time, was awarded the OBE, and even came in as runner-up in the BBC's Sports Personality of the Year competition. But it does not do to be too confident when your life is spent hurtling round a racetrack at hundreds of miles an hour. That year, Hill's teammate James Clark was killed at Hockenheim. Injury and death were at that time constant companions on the racetrack and every time a driver came off the grid he ran a tremendous personal risk. It was only comparatively recently that the use of seatbelts had been encouraged. The next year, it was Hill's turn.

Travelling at 160 mph at Watkins Glen, a tyre collapsed and Graham Hill's car ploughed into an earth bank. As it flipped over, he fell out and landed with full force on his knees, breaking one knee and dislocating the other, as well as tearing the ligaments. He was lucky, he was alive, but his injuries kept him out of action for the rest of 1969 and the first two months of 1970.

His determination to get back to racing drove him on – he even rode a bicycle four miles each way to his physiotherapy sessions. But his old firm, Lotus, were not keen to have a 40-year-old man back, and when he returned to the track at the South African Grand Prix in March, it was with the Rob Walker Racing Team, with later another switch to the Brabham team. And then, in 1972, he achieved another of those victories that made him unique amongst racing drivers – he won the Le Mans 24-Hour race, sharing a car with Henri Pescarolo. By doing so he became the only man to have claimed title to this 'Triple Crown' of Formula One World Championship, Le Mans and the Indianapolis 500.

But there was nothing he could do about the years passing by. He was now 43 years old, and there were too many young stars rising for him to be able to count on being offered a drive. In an effort to put off the inevitable, he set about creating his own

GRAHAM HILL (1929–1975)

racing team, sponsored by W.D. & H.O. Wills under their Embassy brand, but despite some success it was a very frustrating and highly stressful time. The huge amounts of money that were now coming into Formula One had made it a different world from that in which he had begun his career, and he was increasingly aware that he was becoming a 'veteran' rather than a cutting edge competitor. In 1975, at the British Grand Prix at Silverstone, Graham Hill announced his retirement from the track – from now on he would attend meetings only to watch his team cars.

There was a collective sigh of relief when he finally made up his mind to retire. Nobody had wanted to see him carry on long past his prime as a racing driver, not his fans nor his fellow drivers and friends, and certainly not his family. In 1972 they had moved from Mill Hill to 'Lyndhurst', a house on the edge of Shenley village in Hertfordshire – Damon (soon, of course, to be a world champion racing driver himself) was sent to Haberdashers' Aske's school nearby, and it was convenient for Elstree aerodrome. Bette hoped for a more settled life for the family. In fact, she was disappointed that he wanted to continue his association with racing at all – 'I didn't want Graham to build a team.' she said later. 'There wasn't sufficient support or finance. It was the biggest heartbreak and toughest job he ever took on. The saddest thing is he was just getting it together when he had the crash.'

Hill had been flying light aircraft for ten years (he bought the Piper Aztec with the money he won at the Indianapolis 500) and did so with supreme self-confidence – perhaps over-confidence. The investigation following the crash showed that his altimeter had been improperly set, which meant that he was flying lower than he believed himself to be. He would not have been able to see the trees on the golf course through the fog. As a friend said, 'In those conditions it's just a matter of feet and seconds between life and death.' Hill had been defying the odds for years, but nothing could get him out of that situation.

The familiar figure of Graham Hill striding towards his Embassy car.
(Ian Simpson)

On board the plane with Graham Hill was a substantial part of the Embassy-Hill team: team manager Ray Brimble, driver Tony Brise, designer Andy Smallman, and mechanics Terry Richards and Tony Alcock. Afterwards it was found that Hill's pilot's licence was not up to date and insurers refused to pay out, so that relatives of those men had to sue Hill's estate for compensation, a distressing end to a terrible event.

The death of such a charismatic local hero at such a young age was deeply felt. His funeral was held at St Albans Abbey on 5th December 1975, with thousands of people standing in the cold outside to pay their respects. Later, his ashes were taken to St Botolph's churchyard at Shenley.

12

Lady Constance Lytton (1869–1923)

Suffragette martyr

On 24th February 1909, a delicate, well-dressed lady boarded the train at Knebworth Station. She was well known to the station staff and was treated with due deference and attention – she was, after all, the daughter of the 1st Earl Lytton of Knebworth House and the sister of the current Earl. Lady Constance Lytton was on her way to London, and embarking on an adventure that filled her with fear and excitement and that would finally lead to her early death. She was going to join her suffragette friends. She had not even dared to tell her family that she was going, afraid that the news would cause her much-loved mother pain and distress.

Lady Constance was an unlikely recruit to the militant suffragette movement, having all her life suffered from a weak heart and rheumatism that had made her practically an invalid. The third child of Robert, Lord Lytton, the first Earl, and his wife Edith Villiers, she had spent her childhood travelling from country to country, wherever her father's diplomatic work took him, including several years when he was Viceroy of India. For the last four years of his life they were based in Paris, where he died in 1892. Her mother had then been appointed lady-in-waiting to Queen Victoria, and subsequently to Queen Alexandra. In 1905, however, her mother had left Court and retired to Knebworth, where she and Constance lived quietly at 'Homewood', a beautiful house designed and built for them by Constance's brother-in-law, Edwin Lutyens in 1901.

It would have been almost impossible in those years to have had no opinion on the 'woman question'. The fight for female

Lady Constance Lytton. (Terry Pankhurst)

suffrage had already been a long one, fought mostly on men's terms and constitutionally, and it had been unsuccessful. But in the early years of the 20th century a new breed of women were taking matters into their own hands, led by Mrs Emmeline Pankhurst and her two daughters, Sylvia and Christabel, who believed that only direct action would force Parliament to take women seriously. The word 'suffragette' was first coined by the *Daily Mirror* in 1906, to differentiate these militant females from the law-abiding 'suffragists'.

LADY CONSTANCE LYTTON (1869–1923)

In 1908, Lady Constance met Mrs Emmeline Pethwick-Lawrence and Annie Kenney, two of the most famous of Mrs Pankhurst's followers. Constance was a supporter of women's right to the vote but at that time did not agree with the tactics of the militants, which she then thought 'unjustified, unreasonable, without a sense of political responsibility'. But she was impressed by Pethwick-Lawrence and Annie Kenney and by their clear sense of purpose, and her meeting with them changed her life. Later that year, she was at the House of Commons when Mrs Pankhurst was arrested once again and Constance tried to use her influence to help her, unsuccessfully. Mrs Pankhurst and Christabel went to prison, and the newspapers were full of talk of the suffragettes. Lady Constance must have spent the next few months in some mental turmoil, and she wrote later that she had tried to communicate her passionate sense of the injustice of it all to her mother, who did not really want to hear about it. But nothing could now dissuade Constance from the course she had chosen – she had decided to offer herself up for imprisonment too.

When Constance arrived in London that February day, she already had a debilitating headache from the stress of it all but was determined to take her place in prison with the other women of the Women's Social and Political Union (WSPU). Mrs Pethwick-Lawrence was going to lead a deputation to see Prime Minister Asquith at the House of Commons, whether he wanted to see her or not after he had once again scuppered a suffrage bill, and Lady Constance had been accepted as one of the deputation.

As the women got close to Parliament, they were confronted by burly policemen who had no compunction in swatting them out of the way. Lady Constance found herself breathless and dazed, forced to rest for a moment against the shoulder of a complete stranger before she could go on – three times, she recalled, a policeman would 'seize me with both his hands around the ribs, squeeze the remaining breath out of my body and lifting me completely into the air, throw me with all his strength'. It was a violent initiation, and all she had done so far was to try to approach the House of Commons.

Lady Constance was arrested, as she had known she would be, and sentenced to one month's imprisonment. Because of her family connections and her heart condition, she was given special treatment and put into the hospital ward at Holloway Prison instead of into the cells. She hated this differentiation between herself and the rest of the suffragettes, and chose a dreadful way of protesting – she began to draw on her skin with a needle, managing to produce a 'V' as the start of 'Votes for Women' on her chest before she was stopped. At last, she was transferred to the cells with the others.

In October 1909, Lady Constance ('Lady Con', or 'Lady Connie', as she was known to her friends in the movement) was again in prison, and again being given special treatment, this time in Newcastle after she had thrown a stone, rather tentatively, at a car thought to be carrying Lloyd George. But by now the tempo of the conflict had intensified – the force-feeding of hunger-striking imprisoned suffragettes had begun and she listened in prison to the screams of women in agony as they were held down and a tube was forced down their throats. Her shame intensified at the special treatment shown to her because of her name and position.

Quite apart from her support for what she considered the obvious right of women to the vote, Constance had found something with the suffragettes that was very precious to her, a comradeship and unquestioning friendship unlike anything she had experienced before. She was determined that next time she would be treated like everyone else – so she disguised herself as an unattractive working-class woman, Jane Warton, and was arrested at a protest meeting in January 1910 in Liverpool. She was sentenced to two weeks' imprisonment as a first offender and immediately went on hunger strike. This time there was no deferential treatment and she suffered as many women had over the past year. Later, she described her ordeal.

She was held down on a plank bed in her cell by three wardresses, two holding her arms and one her feet. As she would not open her mouth voluntarily, a steel gag was used to prize her jaws wide apart. Then the tube was inserted and pushed down her throat into her stomach. She choked as it went down. The liquid food was poured down the tube, so quickly that it was violently expelled by her body, 'the horror of it was more than I can describe'. She vomited over the wardresses and the doctor and herself, and it seemed an eternity before the tube was drawn out.

Then the doctor 'gave me a slap on the cheek, not violently, but, as it were, to express his contemptuous disapproval'. That slap brought a sudden insight. She seemed to see Jane Warton as others saw her – 'the most despised, ignorant and helpless prisoner that I had seen . . . When she had served her time and was out of the prison, no one would believe anything she said, and the doctor, when he had fed her by force and tortured her body, struck her on the cheek to show how he despised her!' In a moment of almost religious intensity, she understood: 'That was Jane Warton, and I had come to help her.' Left alone in the cell, lying in her vomit, she still had the strength to call out 'No surrender' and was answered by the woman in the next cell, 'No surrender'.

Before her identity was discovered and she was released, Lady Constance was force-fed another seven times.

Her sister, Lady Emily Lutyens, came to get her from Walton Gaol. Her brother the Earl had been alerted to her situation by the newspapers and, as Constance was forced to have complete rest to try to recover her strength, he took up her case and attacked the government's role in her ordeal. But no one was interested, a general election was looming and they had more important matters to think about. Once the election was over, Lord Lytton took Constance's torture up again, this time with his friend Winston Churchill, now Home Secretary. One weekend in April 1910, Churchill stayed at Knebworth House and went through the papers – his verdict: forget it, there's no hope of making a proper complaint against her treatment.

Lord Lytton proved a good friend to the women's suffrage movement. He headed the cross-party Conciliation Committee that backed the Conciliation Bill, which would, if it had ever been passed, have given the vote immediately to over a million women and satisfied the Pankhursts and many others in the suffragette movement. Political manoeuvring killed it, with Asquith, Lloyd George and Winston Churchill speaking against it. And so the suffragettes began the most violent campaign yet seen. The next years would see destruction of property, bombing, and episodes of arson.

Knebworth House in the early 1900s – a far cry from a prison cell.
(Hertfordshire Illustrated Review)

LADY CONSTANCE LYTTON (1869–1923)

Lady Constance had worked hard alongside her brother for the Bill, and in 1910 she suffered a slight stroke. The next year, she was out with the rest of the suffragettes in London, smashing windows to make their point. Sent back to Holloway, she was soon released as her fine was paid anonymously – perhaps her family could not bear for her to suffer again?

In May 1912 she suffered another stroke, her heart irreparably damaged by the violence she had undergone. She was paralysed down her right side, and thus ended her direct involvement in the movement. But she was not to be silenced, and for the next two years she wrote, slowly and with great care, with her left hand, her recollections, published as *Prisons and Prisoners* in 1914. She never recovered her health and lived on quietly at Knebworth, surviving to see the vote granted to women aged 30 and over in 1919. Those eventful five years with the suffragettes had given her a purpose for living that she could never have dreamed of as the earl's invalid daughter. She died on 22nd May 1923, aged 53 years.

13

Dr Arthur Martin-Leake (1874–1953)

The man who won the VC twice

The Victoria Cross is the highest decoration for gallantry that can be awarded to a member of the British and Commonwealth forces, created 'For Valour' by Queen Victoria in 1856 to honour, firstly, brave soldiers of the Crimean War. The criteria for its award are strict and a man who receives the Victoria Cross is indeed a hero.

Hertfordshire has its share of them. Take Private James Osborne of the 2nd Battalion, Northamptonshire Regiment, for instance, who was born in 1857 in Wigginton. During the First Boer War he rescued a fellow soldier, Private Mayes, who was lying wounded and under heavy fire from a party of Boers. Or Edward Barber of Tring, who served during the First World War with the 1st Battalion, The Grenadier Guards. On 12th March 1915, during the battle of Neuve Chappelle, he ran in front of the grenade company to which he belonged into the midst of the enemy, using his grenades with such deadly accuracy that 'when the grenade party reached Private Barber they found him alone and unsupported, with the enemy surrendering all about him', though sadly he was killed later that same day. Or Edward Warner of St Albans, with the 1st Battalion, Bedfordshire Regiment, who was also awarded the VC in 1915 after he had held a trench single-handedly at Hill 60, Ypres against enemy attack, only to die of his wounds and gas poisoning.

These three are just a few of the brave Hertfordshire men whose names are recorded on the Victoria Cross roll of honour and it seems wrong to single out any one man and ignore the rest. But

DR ARTHUR MARTIN-LEAKE (1874–1953)

there is one man whose courage was so exceptional that he won the VC twice – a doctor named Arthur Martin-Leake from East Hertfordshire.

Martin-Leake was born at High Cross on 4th April 1874. His family were well off and had a property there, Marshalls, and by his early twenties young Arthur seemed set on course for a life in medicine. He qualified at University College Hospital in 1898 and took up a job as a medical officer at the local hospital at Hemel Hempstead.

Then events in the wider world imposed themselves on his life. In October 1899 war broke out between Britain and the Boer republics in southern Africa, and Martin-Leake joined the Hertfordshire Company of the Imperial Yeomanry as a Trooper. Later he was able to use his medical expertise as a Surgeon Captain in the South African Constabulary under General Baden-Powell.

Much of the war, after the first few months, was fought in snatches of violence, the Boers being expert guerilla fighters who knew the country so much better than the British soldiers. On 8th February 1902, Surgeon Captain Martin-Leake was with a party of British soldiers at Vlakfontein, south-east of Johannesburg, where a group of more than 40 Boers were keeping them pinned down under heavy fire from about 100 yards away. He went out into the line of fire to try to help the wounded, left lying in the open under the hot sun. He dressed the wounds of one man as well as he could, then made his way, still under fire, to help a badly wounded officer. There was not much he could do for him in the circumstances, but he tried to get the man into a more comfortable position. Three times he was hit by bullets from the Boers, but even then he only gave up when exhaustion from loss of blood overwhelmed him. Water was beginning to run out, but he refused to take a drink until the other wounded men had been served. Shot in his thigh and right hand, he lay with the dead and wounded for hours until help arrived.

Dr Arthur Martin-Leake, VC and Bar.

Surgeon Captain Martin-Leake's courage under fire was recognised with the award of the Victoria Cross, published in the *London Gazette* on 13th May 1902. The South African War ended a few weeks later.

He didn't allow a small thing like being shot to change his life, however. While he was convalescing, he studied for and passed the examinations for the FRCS (Fellow of the Royal College of Surgeons) in 1903. Then, that autumn, he was appointed Chief Medical Officer of the Bengal Nagpur Railway, where he was to

DR ARTHUR MARTIN-LEAKE (1874–1953)

run a hospital for the next 34 years. And that might have been the end of the story, except that he seems to have felt a responsibility for his fellow man, and especially for the cannon fodder of Europe's wars. When in 1912, 'trouble in the Balkans' flared up into war between Turkey and the Balkan states, including Montenegro, he was on leave in England and volunteered for service with the British Red Cross unit within the Montenegran army, seeing action at Scutari and Taraboosh Mountain. King Nicholas of Montenegro recognised his work with the award of the Order of the Montenegran Red Cross.

Back to India went Dr Martin-Leake, but not for long. In 1914, the 'war to end all wars' broke out and from India he answered his country's call for medical men to volunteer for service. He was posted in the rank of Lieutenant to the 5th Field Ambulance, Royal Army Medical Corps, and was soon in the thick of the fighting in Belgium.

The First Battle of Ypres began on 19th October 1914, less than three months after the war had started. The German army was attempting to push through the Allied lines towards the Channel ports, and the British army was moving north through Belgium to try to stop them. They chased the Germans out of Ypres, only 15 miles from Calais, back to the Passchendaele ridge, but reinforcements of fresh young soldiers from Germany, plus a personal visit to the German front line by the Kaiser, bolstered the German retaliation. On 29th October a new German offensive began between Messines and Geluveld in Belgium, followed in November by an attack on the front from Comines to Dixmuide. Only by the incredible courage of the British troops, 58,000 of whom died, was the attack held back, by action such as that at Polygon Wood where British troops fought hand to hand with the enemy amongst the trees and bushes. For many years afterwards, 31st October was remembered as 'Ypres Day'.

The terrible casualties mounted each day of the assault. Under overwhelming German artillery fire and continuous bombardment by shells, the ground shaking with each burst, soldiers suffered unimaginable injuries. Hunger, exhaustion and sheer terror took their toll too. And in the middle of this carnage were the medical staff, non-combatants but up to their eyes in blood and misery.

There was a system for dealing with the wounded in any battle. A wounded soldier would first walk, if he could, or be stretchered to the regimental aid post on the front line, where the medical officer made a quick assessment of his injuries, stopped the bleeding and cleaned the wounds as best he was able, which in the middle of a battle might be very little. A man too badly wounded to survive might be left quietly to die so that others could be more quickly helped. Then the casualty would be sent back to the advance dressing station (ADS), a little way back from the front line, again either on foot or carried by the intrepid stretcher-bearers. Walking wounded usually congregated at a collecting station, outside the tented ADS. During a battle the station was a scene from hell, the doctors and nurses struggling to cope with a continuous flow of bloody bodies. The next stage was the casualty clearing station, in effect a field hospital set up wherever shelter could be found, which might be in a Nissen hut or a commandeered chateau, and here the surgical teams struggled to amputate, cauterise or to save. If he was still alive by then, a soldier would go from there to a base hospital, or straight to the coast to wait for transport home.

It all sounds very organised, but under the conditions of such a battle of that of First Ypres, the location of the front line could move several times in a few days, or even hours, leaving doctors and wounded stranded and likely to be taken as prisoners of war. They were in any case just as much in danger as the rest of the army from shellfire.

Martin-Leake, now 40 years old, was stationed with the Bearer

DR ARTHUR MARTIN-LEAKE (1874–1953)

Division near to Zonnebecke, in an exposed position just to the north of Geluveld, and his actions over the period 29th October to 8th November went well beyond the call of duty. Not only did he face that nightmarish scene of wounded soldiers brought out of the line, which must have dwarfed anything he could have seen in South Africa, but he found himself unable to turn away from those men who were lying in the no man's land between the Allied and the German positions, wounded and unable to move. Over those eleven days, he repeatedly crawled out under fire to rescue those he could see or hear, bringing them back, sometimes to be treated, sometimes to die, but all of them given a chance, thanks to one man's 'conspicuous bravery and devotion to duty'. Dr Arthur Martin-Leake became the first man ever to be awarded a Bar to the Victoria Cross, in effect winning it twice. Only two other men have since equalled his achievement.

In March 1915 he was promoted to Captain and in November to Major, and the same year the British Medical Association awarded him the Gold Medal. Two years later, as the war dragged on, he was given command of a Field Ambulance as acting Lieutenant Colonel, and for his actions while commanding officer of a casualty clearing station he was mentioned in despatches. And then the war was over, and Martin-Leake went back to his job with the Indian railway.

It would be nice to record that he lived happily ever after, but although he married in 1930, his wife succumbed to a tropical disease after only two years and the couple had no children. He came back in his retirement to his childhood home in High Cross in 1937, where he managed the estate and took a keen interest, as President, in the local branch of the Royal British Legion. When the Second World War broke out, he commanded a mobile Air Raid Precaution (ARP) unit at Puckeridge, still keen to do his duty. He died on 22nd June 1953, aged 79. He bequeathed his medals to the Royal Army Medical Corps (RAMC), and they were later given into the care of the National Army Museum.

Dr Arthur Martin-Leake was buried in the churchyard at St John's church, High Cross. Over the years, with no family nearby to tend it, his grave became dilapidated. In 2001 the Combined Cadet Force from Haileybury College helped to restore the grave. They made a pathway to it, put up a plaque recording his exceptional feats, and a memorial service was held there on the anniversary of his first winning the VC in February 1902, attended by, amongst others, representatives from the RAMC, the Territorial Army and the Royal Anglian Regiment. Wreaths were laid on his grave and a lone bugler sounded *Reveille* and the *Last Post*.

In his book *Tommy*, Richard Holmes records a comment made by Dr Martin Littlewood, who knew Martin-Leake during the First World War. At one time in 1917, the two doctors came under shellfire: 'By God, this is dangerous. Run,' said Martin-Leake. As Dr Littlewood recalled: 'Only a very brave man can be a coward.'

———◆———

14

Henry Moore (1898–1986)

Modern England's greatest sculptor

For over 40 years, the world's greatest living sculptor lived and worked in Hertfordshire. From his studios at Perry Green, a small hamlet near Much Hadham, Henry Moore produced some of his best-known and most influential works of art.

Like so much in life, Moore's arrival in Perry Green in 1940, during the Second World War, was unforeseen and unplanned. He had at that time a studio in London, at his home in Hampstead, and another in Kent. He and his wife Irina had driven out to Perry Green to stay with a friend over the weekend, to give themselves a break from the strain of living through the night-after-night bombardment that was the Blitz. Even there, in the depths of rural Hertfordshire, the glow of London burning could be seen on the night skyline.

The visit over, the couple drove back to London, only to find that a bomb had fallen close to their Hampstead studio, causing enough damage to make it difficult for them to continue living there. Back they came to their friend in Hertfordshire and the decision was made to look for a property somewhere in the area of Much Hadham. Not long after, an old farmhouse with the unprepossessing name of Hoglands became available to rent, and subsequently to buy, in the centre of Perry Green.

While Irina Moore moved into Hoglands, Henry still had work to do in London. He was appointed as a war artist and became engaged on his series of *Shelter Drawings*, which were evocative sketches of life underground while bombs fell overhead. Every night when the air raid sirens sounded, hundreds of Londoners headed for the tube stations, where they slept overnight on the platforms. 'It was like a huge city in the bowels of the earth,' Moore recalled, and his drawings of these refugees from the Blitz are both moving and very human.

Moore had already lived through one war. He was born on 30th July 1898 at Castleford, Yorkshire where his father, a miner, was determined that no son of his would work down the pit. Moore therefore had a good education at local schools, and in particular an education in art, thanks to a teacher who saw talent in the young boy. He was said to have decided he wanted to be a sculptor at the age of eleven, when he discovered the works of Michelangelo.

The First World War was beginning as he was ready to leave school, and he worked as a teacher for a time, before enlisting in the Civil Service Rifles, 15th London Regiment in 1917. He fought at the Battle of Cambrai and was gassed – and when he was demobbed in 1919 he made a decision that set the course for the rest of his life when he became the first student of sculpture at Leeds School of Art.

Moore's works in that inter-war period were often shocking to those who saw them – the verdict might be 'revolutionary', but it could just as easily be 'monstrous' or 'barbarous'. Influences on him included black African art, Mexican sculpture, ancient American art, abstract forms, surrealism and all the other 'isms' with which the cutting-edge 1920s and 1930s art world abounded. His first public commission was for London Transport – the *West Wind Relief* decorating their new headquarters above St James's Park tube station – and his first one-man exhibition followed. By the early Thirties he was becoming well known in the artistic world. Oddly enough, it was the sketches of the *Shelter Drawings*, rather than his sculpture, that brought him to the attention of a wider audience, who could probably relate far more easily to their humanity and sympathy.

HENRY MOORE (1898-1986)

Perry Green had proved to be an inspired choice for a home and studio. A cheque for £300 had enabled him to buy the whole farmhouse at Hoglands – this was in payment for his elmwood *Reclining Figure*. Moore later recalled that when this piece was exhibited at the Leicester Galleries in London, the wood gave off a strange smell that led the gallery staff to have the drains checked. 'Undertakers make coffins out of it,' he explained, hence the 'smell of death'.

Hoglands itself remained virtually unchanged while Moore lived there, although as neighbouring land and properties came onto the market over the years, he bought them and ended up with an estate of over 70 acres. Outlying buildings were soon being converted into studios. In the 1950s an additional, larger studio was built on newly purchased land next door, and later still a kind of pre-fabricated studio was put up nearby – made of a metal frame covered with polythene sheeting, so that in the summer the lower polythene skirts could be lifted to let in the air.

The studios he used had to increase in size because as time went on his works became truly monumental. It was very important to him that they be seen outside in relation to the landscape and the sky, rather than indoors in a museum or studio. He would cite the examples of great works such as Stonehenge, or Nelson's Column – what would they be without the panorama of the sky behind them? – or the great periods of Greek or Egyptian art. The land around Hoglands gradually became a sculpture park, where his works could be placed with due reference to what lay around them – including sheep, of which he was extremely fond.

After the Second World War, Moore's reputation grew steadily. The Museum of Modern Art in New York staged a retrospective exhibition for him in 1946 – the first for an English artist – and American museums and collectors 'discovered' him. Perhaps more importantly, 1946 also saw the birth of his daughter and only child, Mary.

Moore's sculpture of 'Mother and Child: Block Seat'.
(reproduced by permission of the Henry Moore Foundation)

The theme of 'mother and child' ran through much of his work now, which became more approachable though still rather puzzling to the non-artistically minded. These huge, strange figures, often with holes in them, were still emphatically 'modern art' and a closed book to many people – yet to Moore himself, art was simply a way of 'man expressing his response to life'. 'Sculptors are obsessed with shape and the space within it – for that is shape too,' he explained. He wanted to make people look at things in a new way, that they would otherwise never have considered. Whether his original inspiration sprang from natural things such as rocks, bones or plants, or from the human form, it was always something already to be found in everyday life. He once said that much of his inspiration sprang from the curving shape of his mother's hip.

HENRY MOORE (1898–1986)

When he started out on his career, he would begin by producing drawings, refined until they had reached the point at which he could go forward to the next stage of producing a small sketch model, and then a work cast in bronze. Later, he began by working on a three-dimensional maquette, or model, of the work and gradually scaling it up until it reached the final form – working on such small scale to begin with meant that he could discard a piece without concern if it did not seem to be working out. As he became older, and the size of his sculptures increased too, his work involved more people, each helping to progress the model on to the next stage. His studio must then have resembled a medieval master painter's workshop, with the master overseeing but allowing the studio artists to fill in certain parts of the finished work.

Henry Moore received awards, prizes, honours and commissions from all over the world in the next few decades. He was made a Companion of Honour in 1955 and awarded the Order of Merit in 1963 – awards he was pleased to accept from the Queen, although he turned down the offer of a knighthood. Works of his stand today in prestigious spots in many countries, from the marble *Reclining Figure* outside the UNESCO headquarters in Paris to the bronze *Knife Edge Two Piece* outside the Houses of Parliament in London, and honours were showered on him from other countries. An exhibition in 1972 in Florence was only one of many, but the praise expressed by Italian artists and statesmen in that land of Michelangelo must have been especially gratifying. New York, Madrid, Hong Kong, Japan, Ontario – the list of places clamouring to show his works simply went on and on. Every collection, public or private, of any distinction, would have its piece, or pieces, by Henry Moore – and Moore was generous in his gifts to galleries and museums, including the Tate Gallery, the British Museum and the Victoria and Albert Museum.

HERTFORDSHIRE HEROES

Little Perry Green became used to the artistic lion in its midst, the occasional flying visit by a foreign statesman, and the huge strange shapes that could be glimpsed in Hoglands' park from the footpaths nearby. In 1972 Moore established the Henry Moore Trust to prevent his estate and collection being broken up after his death; the Henry Moore Foundation followed in 1976 and in a short while Moore had officially given all his land, studios and works to the Foundation, which has as its aims the conservation of Moore's reputation and work, as well as to assist the arts in general and promote sculpture. His studios and the sculpture park can still be visited today.

Henry Moore, one of the few people who can be called a true 'cultural phenomenon', died on 31st August 1986, at the age of 88. He was buried at St Thomas's church, Perry Green. Perry Green's mother church, St Andrew's at Much Hadham, had benefited from his work over the years. If you visit, be sure to note the heads at each side of the main door, and the stained-glass window installed in 1995 – delicate and understated work that contrasts with the bold sculptures at the Foundation.

15

Eric Morecambe (1926–1984)

A comic genius

On Christmas Night 1977, 29 million people settled down in front of the television with pleasurable anticipation to watch what had become the highlight of festive viewing – the *Morecambe and Wise Christmas Special*. Today, no comedian could hope to engage the attention of half the population of the country at one time. But then, true comic genius does not brighten our world very often and we knew it when we saw it. And with all due respect to that consummate straight man, Ernie Wise, it was the tall one with glasses who was our hero of comedy.

The scripts and the gags were good, but Eric Morecambe also had the gift of being able to make us laugh simply by being there. An adjustment of his trademark spectacles, a gormless sideways grin at the camera, a trick with a paper bag and an invisible 'something' – it doesn't translate well into print, but whatever it is that makes somebody immediately funny, Eric had it in spades. 'Funny bones', perhaps.

The journey from an anonymous working-class home in Morecambe, Lancashire to a detached luxury house in the prosperous Hertfordshire village of Harpenden was not made overnight, or without pain, however. It began on 14th May 1926, when John Eric Bartholomew was born, the son of a Morecambe Corporation labourer. He was an only child and, it soon became apparent, a born performer, happy from a very early age to entertain his family and friends and make people laugh. His mother, Sadie, had ideas of him becoming the second George Formby, a Northern comedian who was then a film and radio idol, and pushed Eric into performing in local clubs from his early teens. His natural gift for laughter endeared him even to those tough audiences – and those were hard times for many in the North, as the Depression cut deep and led to unemployment and hardship.

In 1939, aged just thirteen, he met a young stage and radio performer named Ernest Wiseman, who was already a seasoned 'pro'. As the Second World War began, the two teenagers toured in a show called *Youth takes a Bow*, and became friends. They discovered a delight in the same kind of humour, which seemed to lead naturally to a double act and they made their debut together on stage in 1941 at the Liverpool Empire, though it was 1943 before they officially became 'Morecambe and Wise'. Eric had decided to take the name of his hometown as his professional credit.

It was not easy for any young comedian trying to break into the big time. A couple of years later, the war over at last, ex-servicemen began returning home and some of them were performers whose acts and talents had been honed by experience. When those ex-servicemen included people like Peter Sellers, Eric Sykes, Tommy Cooper, Benny Hill, Tony Hancock and many more, it was obvious that only exceptional talent would make it through in peacetime Britain.

But nothing can faze young men who are sure of themselves and Eric and Ernie were tenacious in their pursuit of success. They began to appear regularly on radio in 1952, and then cast their eye on the new medium of television. Hard to imagine now, but television was just beginning to make its mark in Britain's homes, boosted by the transmission live of the Coronation in 1953 – and until 1955, when ITV was born, there was only one channel available. In 1954 Morecambe and Wise had their first BBC television series, *Running Wild*. It was not an auspicious start and was slated by the critics, one of whom (Mark Johns of the *Daily*

Eric Morecambe

Sketch) said that 'their gags were weak, their sketches corny'. It was a depressing time, but Eric was helped through it by the unswerving support of his wife, Joan, and the birth of their children, Gail in 1953 and Gary in 1956.

After that setback, they returned for a time to what they knew best. Stage work and the rapport they could create with a live audience reinvigorated them. Johnny Speight, who wrote for them at that time, still thought they were 'television naturals', and they began to make regular appearances in guest spots on other people's shows. Television, they felt, was definitely the future.

In 1961 the *Morecambe and Wise Show* made its first appearance on ATV, along with *Two of a Kind*, the first song to be associated with them. Here were the characters we came to love

– 'Eric & Ern', one with glasses and one with short, fat, hairy legs. Their own talents, aided by the writing of Dick Hills and Sid Green and the production of Colin Clews, together with star guests such as the Beatles, made them household names. Award after award followed, with their first BAFTA award in 1963, and perhaps an even greater accolade the following year when they were invited to perform at Windsor Castle before the Royal Family.

It was also in 1961 that Eric and his family moved to Harpenden in Hertfordshire, then a quieter and more rural community than it is today. It was also a long way from the studios, compared with their London home, but as Eric put it: 'I don't mind the commuting, it's the travelling that gets me down.'

Eric had always been a worrier, always on the move, with a tendency to overwork if he could. 'Jifflearse' was his mother's name for him. Now he was smoking up to a hundred cigarettes a day, overjoyed by success but almost obsessively worried that everything was going too well to be true and that it would all end tomorrow. And make no mistake, it was hard work staying at the top. By 1966 their weekly show was being watched in over 8 million homes and they were travelling all over the country making personal appearances, as well as appearing in the pop charts with hit singles such as *Boom Oo Yatta-Ta-Ta!* One dream, though, was never realised, and that was to take their success to America. Despite appearances on the *Ed Sullivan Show*, their humour did not travel and they never made the breakthrough they (particularly Ernie) hoped for.

However, another great ambition – to make it on the big screen – was achieved. In three years, beginning in 1965, three Morecambe and Wise films hit the cinemas – *The Intelligence Men*, *That Riviera Touch*, and *The Magnificent Two*. It was hugely exciting for both Eric and Ernie to stargaze at Pinewood Studios and they put their hearts into the new venture, but Rank did not give them the investment they deserved and the films were greeted with

ERIC MORECAMBE (1926-1984)

mixed reviews. Later, both Eric and Ernie came to regret the lost opportunity that was their foray into cinema – in 1983 they made a further film, *Night Train to Murder*, but it was not a success.

In 1968, Morecambe and Wise moved from ITV after a row with Lew Grade, to Bill Cotton at the BBC, and so began the period that saw them at the very peak of their profession. But not before Eric's hectic and stressful lifestyle caught up with him. On 7th November 1968 he suffered his first heart attack, an attack so serious that for a while it seemed he might never recover, let alone work again. Typically, he made light of the event. Alone and ill in his car in Leeds at one o'clock in the morning, the only person he could attract the attention of was a complete stranger who, he discovered, had been in the Territorial Army. 'He drove my [Jensen] car like a tank for miles. Then he had to wake someone at the hospital. Finally as they wheeled me into intensive care I saw him bending over me. He whispered in my ear, "Can I have your autograph before you go?"'

Morecambe and Wise were national treasures by this time and Eric's progress was followed with concern by millions. When he reappeared on television, on 27th July 1969, it was to rapturous applause – particularly for the remark, 'Keep going, you fool!' directed at his chest as he strode to the front of the stage.

The BBC shows, scripted by Eddie Braben, have become part of television folklore. Millions of people watched and laughed together, and the Christmas specials were events to be savoured for weeks beforehand. Great stars such as André Previn, Glenda Jackson, Laurence Olivier, Shirley Bassey, Rudolf Nureyev and so many more, queued up to appear with, and be made fun of by Morecambe and Wise. Again award after award came their way. From 1974 Ernest Maxin produced the show, and introduced the Hollywood dance sequences, including *Singing in the Rain* and that marvellous routine of preparing breakfast to *The Stripper*.

For reasons never made clear, in 1978 Morecambe and Wise

Eric and Ernie at work

left the BBC and went back to ITV. It was not a successful move, but was eclipsed in importance when in March 1979 Eric suffered his second heart attack. He was rushed from Harpenden to St Albans City Hospital, and made a good recovery, but in May he underwent a triple by-pass operation at Harefield Hospital.

It was enough to slow anyone down, even 'Jifflearse', and an increased awareness of the fragility of life and of the many separations his family had had to endure over the years made Eric decide to spend more time at home with those he loved. He couldn't be idle for long, though, and took up writing; his novel *Mr Lonely* was published in 1981.

He was back on TV a year after the operation, but by now he

ERIC MORECAMBE (1926–1984)

found the old routine a boring treadmill. His home at Harpenden, his friends and his hobbies, including fishing, birdwatching, photography and writing, had become more important to him and the old enjoyment had gone. But 40 years of show business, and the responsibility of being half of a double act, made it difficult for him to know what to do next.

By 1984 Eric was ready to retire. That April he began to feel unwell, and was due to go back to Harefield for tests, but he had a couple of engagements to attend first – a friend's wedding, and a charity appearance at a small theatre in Tewkesbury. The wedding went off well, and the next day, Sunday, he and Joan travelled to the Roses Theatre at Tewkesbury, where he seemed happy and relaxed and gave a great performance.

Coming off stage, Eric collapsed in the wings. He was taken to Cheltenham General Hospital but this time nothing could be done. He died just before 4 am on Monday, 28th May 1984.

There was nationally a huge sense of loss, but especially in his home village of Harpenden. He had always been willing to help out with personal appearances at charity or community events, he had played golf at the local club, shopped in the local high street, and given the village many a mention in his comedy routines. Everyone in the land knew that he supported (was a director of) Luton Football Club just up the road.

On the morning of Monday, 4th June 1984, over 1,000 people gathered silently outside St Nicholas' church in the centre of Harpenden. They were there to pay their last respects to a man who had a unique place in our hearts. Of course, there were tributes from some of the biggest stars in British show business. But there were also flowers from the staff of Boots the Chemist in the High Street, and from the local Chinese restaurant. Eric may have been born in the North, but over twenty years he had become very much a 'local' lad. The song with which Morecambe and Wise ended their later shows was *Bring Me Sunshine*. Perhaps the most representative of the floral tributes at his funeral was a simple bunch of pansies, sent anonymously but which surely spoke for millions of people – 'Thank you for the sunshine'.

———◆———

16

William Leefe Robinson (1895–1918) and Wulstan J. Tempest (1891–1966)

Our Zeppelin heroes

From parts of Hertfordshire, you could have had a ringside seat for the Zeppelin raids on London in the First World War. At Hertford Heath, for instance, the vicar's family 'would walk up to a high point where the long horizon could be seen lit up by continuous flashes and flickers, as the anti-aircraft guns kept up their barrage . . . Then, as searchlight after searchlight shot its great arm of light into the sky . . . we knew the Zepp was near.' There was a kind of deadly beauty about that silver shape cruising through the sky, seemingly invincible, but by the beginning of September 1916 English nerves, already raw from two years of war, were stretched tight on a 'Zepp night'.

The Zeppelins, the great cigar-shaped airships perfected as a weapon by the Germans and which far outperformed any British competitor, had been bringing the war to England for over a year by then, since Norfolk villages had been bombed for the first time from the air in January 1915. As the war in France became bogged down on the Western Front, the German High Command turned to weapons that could be sent silently deep into enemy territory – the U-boat under the sea and the Zeppelin in the air. On 8th September 1915, London itself had been bombed for the first time with high explosives and incendiaries, leaving Londoners shocked, frightened and angry.

The anger was directed against the 'murdering Hun', of course, but also against the hapless Royal Flying Corps pilots, who had been unable to defend the capital of the British Empire from attack. They had neither the equipment, the techniques, nor the organisation to do so – yet. Repeated Zeppelin raids over the next year, from London to Liverpool and Tyneside, with more lives lost and property damaged, led to Kitchener's demand that the RFC find a way to deal with them. But, a year after that first raid on London, civilians were still waiting for a modern St George to confront and destroy the mocking Hun. Invariably a raid on London brought the Zepps over Hertfordshire and on 13th October 1915 a departing Zeppelin dropped bombs on unprotected Hertford. Nine people died and fifteen were injured. For Hertfordshire folk, this had become personal.

The night of Saturday, 2nd September 1916 was perfect Zepp-raiding weather – dark, no moon, low cloud and enough ground mist to handicap defending aircraft. The air had been humming with wireless messages since midday and at nine o'clock in the evening an air raid warning was sent out to the home defence posts. The lightships anchored offshore in the North Sea were the first to see the Zeppelin convoy, then they passed over Norfolk, and Essex, and on over Hertfordshire, heading for London. The throbbing drone of their engines and the occasional dull thump of exploding bombs woke up the dark countryside yet again for miles around. Just after eleven o'clock, the duty pilots at the three grass airfields around London were sent up to patrol. At Sutton's Farm, near Hornchurch, that meant Lieutenant William Leefe Robinson, of B Flight, No 39 Squadron Home Defence Wing, a 21-year-old veteran, known as 'Robby' to his friends.

The pilots who went up to face the enemy were on their own once they left the airfield. Freezing cold in the open cockpit of the BE2c biplane – a fragile-looking craft that was prone to engine failure – they had no radios, no sophisticated gadgetry to help them, just a minimum of weaponry that they had to operate themselves while at the same time flying the plane in difficult situations. Against the awesome might of the Zeppelins, which had shrugged off whatever had been aimed at them so far, they resembled a mosquito attacking an elephant. But the courage of the pilots was equal to the challenge. And on this night, at last, Robinson had a new weapon he was eager to try out – incendiary bullets, mixed with tracer so that it could be seen in the dark. As he climbed into the night air (the BE2c took an hour to reach 10,000 ft) and heard the crump and rumble of bombs falling to the north of London, and the spitting of the anti-aircraft guns, he was excited and eager for the confrontation.

First he had to find the Zepp. He had been in the air for nearly two hours when at last he saw it, balanced in a searchlight beam. As quickly as he spotted it, it had vanished into the clouds. But three-quarters of an hour later, he saw it again – the Schutte Lanz SL.11, which had dropped bombs on London Colney and North Mimms before attacking London.

Robinson headed straight for it. He needed to get under the belly of the elephant if he was to have any chance of success, and he wanted that success very badly. One pass, then another, firing the new bullets straight into the body of the Zepp. Nothing. He came around again, this time concentrating his fire in one area. And then he saw a red glow under the skin of the airship that told him he had, finally, done it.

Below, Londoners thronging the streets cheered and danced as the Zeppelin burst into flames. The huge ball of fire lit up the night sky like a new sun, and could be seen quite plainly over 30 miles away. Nose first, the crumbling wooden framework dived to earth – and Robinson felt its deadly heat as he desperately wrenched his plane out of its way. The problem with attacking from below was that you were in the direct line of tons of burning wreckage. He fired off all his Very lights in celebration and headed for home, exhausted, cold and shocked, but happy. At last, a Zeppelin had been shot down over British soil.

In the little village of Cuffley, people had been woken earlier

William Leefe Robinson (left) and Wulstan Tempest in the uniform of the Royal Flying Corps.

by the familiar sound of the Zeppelin as it passed over. Now the searingly bright light was heading straight for them. By great good fortune, the SL.11 missed the village and plunged into a field behind the Plough inn, where it burned for another two hours. The charred bodies of the crew were recovered and taken into St Andrew's church nearby.

A thunderstorm at dawn heralded a wet, miserable day, but nothing could have deterred the thousands of people who walked, rode cycles and motorbikes, drove cars, rode on horseback, or came by taxi or train to Cuffley to see for themselves the mighty fallen SL.11. They came from London and beyond, and from all over Hertfordshire, so many of them that some went away again without ever having got close enough to actually see anything – it didn't matter, what was important was to have been 'there'.

WILLIAM ROBINSON & WULSTAN TEMPEST

Lieut. Robinson was England's, not just Hertfordshire's, hero. He was promoted to captain and invited to Windsor to receive the Victoria Cross from King George V. Tangible rewards came his way too, such as the £4,250 he collected for being the first to shoot down a Zepp over England. Charming, handsome, fair-haired and blue-eyed, he must have seemed the very image of the gallant Englishman overcoming overwhelming odds – a St George indeed. It all became rather too much for him in the end and he asked for, and received, a transfer away from London to a squadron readying itself for France.

The German aircrew were buried hastily, though with due consideration from the RFC for fellow servicemen, in the cemetery at Potters Bar, on the Wednesday after they had been shot down. Local feeling was still running high, not least because the Zeppelin raid had had fatal consequences elsewhere in Hertfordshire.

Having seen their companion, SL.11, shot down in flames, the other Zeppelins in the convoy that Saturday night had turned for home. One jettisoned its bombs as it went, bringing terror to Essendon, a small village outside Hertford. Cottages in the centre of the village were damaged, part of the centuries-old parish church was demolished, and two sisters were killed: 26-year-old Frances Bamford was killed outright and her eleven-year-old sister Eleanor died from her wounds. The girls were buried together in the village churchyard the same day as the German crew were interred at Potters Bar.

The Zeppelins were invincible no longer and the RFC's revenge gathered pace through September. Two more were brought down in Essex and then, on the night of 1st October, it was Hertfordshire's turn once again. It might have been thought an anti-climax to Robinson's epic feat, but to the airmen themselves this was the big one – the L.31 commanded by Captain Heinrich Mathy, who held a reputation amongst Zeppelin commanders similar to that of the Baron von Richthoven ('the Red Baron') amongst pilots on the Western Front. Any pilot would have given his eyeteeth to claim Mathy's Zeppelin. The lot fell to Lieutenant Wulstan Tempest, from the same patrol at Sutton's Farm as Leefe Robinson.

Tempest was duty pilot when the air raid warning came in and was soon flying on patrol over London. The pilots had been, unofficially, trying out ideas to help give them an advantage in attack and Tempest decided to forget regulations and chuck out everything but one Lewis gun and the ammunition. Thus lightened, his plane could reach a higher altitude, closer to that of the Zeppelins.

It was another clear, cold night, pierced by searchlight beams which gradually concentrated in one spot about fifteen miles from Tempest's position, where a Zepp, seeming at that distance 'no bigger than a dart', hovered. Tempest headed for it, through the anti-aircraft fire coming from below. When Mathy saw him coming, he jettisoned his bombs in an attempt to gain height and speed – they fell mostly on open ground but damaged houses in Cheshunt.

Then, Tempest said later, it was just the two of them – Mathy and he – alone in the cool darkness. Suddenly, Tempest's petrol pressure pump failed, and he had to go through the attack while using the hand pump to keep his engine going. Like Robinson before him, he seemed to make no impact with his explosive bullets at first, but then there was a red glow, 'like an immense Chinese lantern'. Then Tempest underwent his own heart-stopping moment as he corkscrewed his plane out of the way of the falling Zepp.

The physical and mental effort had left Tempest dizzy and completely exhausted – for a while he had no idea what had happened or where he was. He made it back down, crash-landing at North Weald Bassett airfield, and shrugging off the fractured skull he suffered.

Déjà vu on the ground, as another blazing wreck plummeted to earth, but this time it was the inhabitants of Potters Bar who watched with growing alarm. Luck held again, as the Zeppelin fell in fields away from the village, at Oakmere Farm. Some of the crew had burned with their craft, others had chosen to jump to certain death rather than burn. Heinrich Mathy was one of those who had jumped, and his body was quickly recognised. A barn nearby was turned into a temporary mortuary, as once again sightseers descended on the area. The authorities were better prepared this time, however, and by 2 a.m. the site had been sealed off and was under guard.

Robinson's Zepp had been a Schutte Lanz airship (technically not a Zeppelin) and its wooden frame had burned away to almost nothing. Tempest's prize, however, was now a smouldering pile of aluminium wreckage, twenty ft high. Souvenir hunters were out in force again, but were quickly cracked down on by the authorities.

The crew were buried next to the men of SL.11 in Potters Bar cemetery. Mathy was given a separate grave, as befitted his status. It wasn't the end, but the worst of the Zeppelin terror was over.

Almost twenty years later, in the early 1930s, the German graves became the focus of so-called Heroes Days, when representatives of the German air service and government came to Potters Bar cemetery to salute their fallen comrades. This led to the curious sight of the swastika of Hitler's Germany being held aloft in an English graveyard and became increasingly irritating to a growing number of people as war again became a terrifying possibility. The last Heroes Day was held in February 1939, attended by the German Ambassador, von Ribbentrop. In 1964 the German airmen's remains were removed and reinterred at Cannock Chase memorial cemetery.

And what of our heroes? Wulstan Tempest, DSO, MC, survived

the war, serving with, and eventually commanding, the night-bombing No 100 Squadron on the Western Front. He left the RAF in 1921, and died in 1966. The area where 'his' Zepp crashed was built over as Oakmere Park, and Tempest Avenue was named in his honour.

The war of William Leefe Robinson, VC, was very different. Shot down in France, he was taken a prisoner of war and suffered ill treatment at the hands of his guards. He tried to escape three times but was recaptured, and by the time he was repatriated he was already ill. He tragically succumbed to the influenza epidemic that swept the world, and died at the age of 23 on 31st December 1918. In 1921 an obelisk was erected to his memory at Cuffley, paid for by readers of the *Daily Express* newspaper.

17

George Bernard Shaw (1856–1950)

Playwright, philosopher and wit

He was perhaps the first 20th-century superstar, known to millions around the world simply by his initials, 'GBS'. Playwright, philosopher, socialist and wit, George Bernard Shaw's new plays and other works were eagerly awaited on every continent for five decades, and thousands of letters from his admirers of every nationality found their way to the quiet Hertfordshire village he made his home.

George Bernard Shaw was born in 1856 in Dublin. He had a rather unhappy childhood, not through ill treatment but because he was simply ignored by both his father, George Shaw, who was an alcoholic, and his mother, Lucinda, who was more interested in the music that she made with her lover, George Lee. Perhaps not surprisingly, he came to dislike the name George intensely and was known by his second name, Bernard. He seems always to have had the conviction, however, that he was destined for great things, and after moving to London at the age of twenty he began on the literary path that was to lead him to life-long fame.

Shaw once remarked that he decided to settle in Ayot St Lawrence after he read a memorial inscription on a gravestone in the village churchyard. '*In loving remembrance of Mary Ann South, who died in London and was brought here to rest by her children*', it read, '*Born March 5 1825 – Died February 13 1895. In the midst of life we are in death. Her time was short.*' Shaw felt that any community where 70-year-olds were considered short-lived was the place for him. Although he always kept up a flat in London, he moved into the New Rectory in Ayot in 1906 and was to

George Bernard Shaw

remain a village inhabitant for the next 44 years until his death at the age of 94 in 1950, thus outliving Mary Ann and proving himself right – as he would no doubt have been the first to point out.

When Shaw arrived in Ayot St Lawrence he was already an accomplished and fashionably lauded playwright. His many

GEORGE BERNARD SHAW (1856–1950)

works included *Major Barbara, Caesar and Cleopatra, Mrs Warren's Profession, Arms and the Man,* and *Man and Superman,* while in the years after settling at Shaw's Corner (as the New Rectory soon became known), he was to go on to add *Pygmalion, Androcles and the Lion, Heartbreak House, Back to Methuselah* and *Saint Joan* – a bare few of the enormous number of works he completed in his lifetime, this man who never stopped writing, even into his nineties. Several of his works were made into popular films and he won an Oscar in 1938 for the screenplay of *Pygmalion,* starring Wendy Hiller and Leslie Howard (the plot of *Pygmalion* was later used for the musical *My Fair Lady,* filmed starring Audrey Hepburn in 1964). Honours were not sought by him. In 1926 he was awarded the Nobel Prize for Literature, a weighty honour indeed, but Shaw refused to accept the £7,000 prize money and instead had it put towards the foundation of an Anglo-Swedish Literary Foundation.

At the heart of many of his greatest works was his total commitment to socialist principles. He was perhaps one of the most famous socialists in the world and wrote, and spoke, with the intention of stirring people to think and argue about ideas, society and religion. He used wit and humour to coat the pill and created fictional characters to bring ideas to life but as he explained, 'All Shaw's characters are himself.'

That commitment to socialism did not, though, prevent him from taking a healthy interest in the financial worth of his writings. When in 1946 the film of his play *Caesar and Cleopatra* was shown at Welwyn, Shaw paid for a seat in the cinema, despite the manager offering to let him in free – after all, the manager insisted, the cinema staff themselves saw the film for nothing. 'Yes,' was the reply, 'but they don't get ten per cent on it. I do.'

In some ways, 'GBS' seems to have been a role he deliberately took on, creating a personality that would shield his own rather more sensitive and shy self, but he did it with gusto, making full use of the press and new inventions of the 20th century like radio, film and later television. People wrote to him in their thousands, sending manuscripts or ideas for advice, asking for money, arguing with him, requesting an autograph, telling him about something important in their own lives, or simply wanting to communicate with someone whom they felt they knew personally. Letters addressed simply 'GBS, England', would find their way to Ayot St Lawrence thanks to the Royal Mail, via their sorting office at Welwyn Garden City, who must have looked upon the challenge as something akin to finding 'Father Christmas, Lapland'. Harry Rayner, the village postman, was a familiar figure at the door of Shaw's Corner.

Shaw said that he could have written another twenty plays in the time it took him to answer his correspondence – not surprisingly, as it has been estimated that during his adult life he wrote an amazing quarter of a million letters and postcards. Even so, a Shaw autograph was worth a few pounds on the collectors' market even in his own lifetime – a fact that made him wary of responding to pleas from autograph hunters. His huge correspondence meant that the post office at Ayot must have been one of the busiest for its size in the county. He made a point of always buying his stamps there, which helped to boost the income of the postmistress, Mrs Jisbella Lyth.

Shaw's incredible personal fame was largely encompassed by his 'GBS' persona, but the villagers of Ayot St Lawrence and the surrounding Hertfordshire countryside knew him as a man who was simply a good neighbour. 'Mr Shaw' was a well-known figure in the lanes, riding his bike, dressed in Victorian knickerbockers and with those distinctive whiskers flying (in his later years he progressed to a tricycle). One local man recalled that he rode into St Albans market every week, where this dedicated vegetarian parked his bike quite deliberately up against a butcher's shop window in St Peter's Street, obscuring its meaty display from view and infuriating the butcher.

His works and witticisms gave the world the impression that Shaw was a confirmed atheist, but that did not stop him supporting the church at Ayot – 'Christians could not wish for a more kindly fellow-traveller,' said the rector, Revd R.J. Davies. Shaw contributed to the repairs to the church roof, paid for the restoration of the organ, and even paid 'pew rent' to boost church funds. Reverend Davies was at Shaw's bedside before he died.

The wrought iron gates at Shaw's Corner were made by a local blacksmith, Mr Westwood of Wheathampstead, in 1948. They not only marked out the house for visitors, but also allowed anyone outside the grounds to see the house. Shaw's Corner had become famous, and welcomed distinguished visitors from all over the world, though Shaw would not allow all uninvited guests through his door. Those who did enter came from the worlds of politics, religion, show business, literature – or were simply people Shaw found interesting. In one week just a year before his death, guests included such diverse characters as Pandit Nehru, the Indian Prime Minister, and Danny Kaye, the American film star. Two men who earlier became friends and frequent visitors were T.E. Lawrence, 'Lawrence of Arabia', and Apsley Cherry-Garrard (see Chapter 6).

Shaw was an extraordinarily attractive man even in old age, tall, with twinkling, mischievous blue eyes and great Irish charisma. Some people saw in him a father figure, many women found him attractive in an altogether different way. His flirtations were usually conducted, however, by post; he carried on a postal love affair with the actress Ellen Terry, for years – the perfect situation, he said, 'She got tired of five husbands but she never got tired of me'. All with the knowledge of his wife, Charlotte, whom he had married in 1898 and with whom he was perfectly happy. He called her his 'green-eyed millionairess' and she called him, simply, 'the genius'. Charlotte's death in September 1943 was a hard blow.

On 10th September 1950, at the age of 94, Shaw fell in his garden at Ayot St Lawrence and broke his thigh, typically while up a ladder attempting to prune a tree. He was taken to Luton & Dunstable Hospital, which rapidly became the focus of media attention from around the world. He came home on 4th October, but was never to recover and he died peacefully on the misty morning of 2nd November 1950. Reporters were waiting at the gates of Shaw's Corner for the news, which was brought to them by Shaw's housekeeper, Mrs Alice Laden. A handwritten notice was later posted on the gates: 'Mr Bernard Shaw passed peacefully away at one minute to five o'clock this morning. From the coffers of his genius, he enriched the world.'

The lanes around Ayot were already blocked by the cars of those who came to mourn the great man, and tributes began to pour in. His great age meant that he was a fixture in public life, many people unable to recall a time when GBS was not there, with his acerbic wit and readiness to weigh in for an argument. He was, quite simply, irreplaceable.

On the day of his funeral, Mrs Lyth drew the shutters and closed the Ayot St Lawrence post office as a mark of respect, the first time in sixteen years it had not been open. The evening before, many villagers had attended their own personal memorial service in the village church. Shaw was cremated at Golders Green crematorium, and his ashes were later mixed with those of his wife, Charlotte, and scattered together in the grounds at Shaw's Corner. In 1944, Shaw had given the house to the National Trust and today visitors from all over the world still come to see this 'living shrine' to one man's prodigious lifetime's work.

Index

HERTFORDSHIRE HEROES